Still Here

Still Here

*Bearing the Weight of Lay Ministry
in a Disaffiliated World*

Andrew Reyes

RESOURCE *Publications* • Eugene, Oregon

STILL HERE
Bearing the Weight of Lay Ministry in a Disaffiliated World

Copyright © 2025 Andrew Reyes. All rights reserved. Except for brief quotations in critical publications or reviews, no part of this book may be reproduced in any manner without prior written permission from the publisher. Write: Permissions, Wipf and Stock Publishers, 199 W. 8th Ave., Suite 3, Eugene, OR 97401.

Resource Publications
An Imprint of Wipf and Stock Publishers
199 W. 8th Ave., Suite 3
Eugene, OR 97401

www.wipfandstock.com

PAPERBACK ISBN: 979-8-3852-5808-6
HARDCOVER ISBN: 979-8-3852-5809-3
EBOOK ISBN: 979-8-3852-5810-9

VERSION NUMBER 11/10/25

For Sheila, Cecy, and Belen—
the first in the trenches with me,
who will recognize more than a few stories in these pages.
And for you, dear friend, who are still here.

Contents

Part I: What We've Inherited

Introduction | 3
Chapter 1: Ministry Without Authority | 23
Chapter 2: The Optics of Engagement | 32
Chapter 3: Culture of Substitution | 41
Chapter 4: Good Enough to Run It, Not Enough to Change It | 49

Accompaniment Meditation I | 57

Part II: What They're Really Leaving

Chapter 5: Beyond Performance-Based Belonging | 65
Chapter 6: Listening to What Disaffiliation Is Really Saying | 74
Chapter 7: Institutional Silence | 82

Accompaniment Meditation II | 90

Part III: What We're Really Called To

Chapter 8: Ministry as Accompaniment, Not Management | 97
Chapter 9: Giving Away the Keys | 103
Chapter 10: You Can't Program Formation | 111
Chapter 11: Burned Out or Burning Bright? | 119

Conclusion: Still Here | 125

Accompaniment Meditation III | 130

Bibliography | 139

Part I

What We've Inherited

Introduction

THE RETREAT THAT DIDN'T HAPPEN

AT 2:15 P.M., I stood beside a school van parked behind the gym, waiting for students to arrive for a junior retreat. The group was small—just seven students—but I believed it could still be meaningful. In fact, I was quietly hopeful. Smaller retreats often allow for more focused conversations, deeper listening, and the kind of vulnerability larger groups sometimes inhibit. I had seen it before: a quiet student opening up during small-group prayer or a retreat talk that landed in a way it never could have among forty restless peers. The intimacy of a smaller group could become a gift—if the group actually showed up.

I stood there with the keys in my hand, the van already unlocked, water bottles neatly packed in the back, and a bag of retreat materials—name tags, journals, prayer guides—waiting to be used. I had printed the small-group assignments earlier that morning, just in case someone showed up late or tried to drop out last-minute. Everything was prepared meticulously, not out of mere habit, but because I believed in the dignity of preparedness. The details mattered. They always did.

I glanced down at my watch, saw the minute hand ticking slowly past the fifteen-minute mark. I reassured myself silently: teenagers run late, maybe they were saying goodbye to friends, maybe they were stopping by their locker, maybe someone needed the bathroom before departure. I scanned the empty parking lot

Part I: What We've Inherited

again, scanning hopefully for any sign of movement—still nothing. Then one student showed up.

He walked toward me slowly, backpack slung casually over one shoulder, his gaze uncertain. He looked apologetic, as if he already sensed something was wrong. "Hey, am I early?" he asked quietly. I smiled, probably a bit too broadly, masking my growing concern. "No, you're right on time," I said reassuringly, feeling the weight of my optimism starting to falter. "We're just waiting for the others."

We stood together in silence for several long moments, the afternoon sun gently warming the pavement beneath our feet, shadows stretching softly across the van. I took out my phone, beginning to dial numbers, though already feeling the futility settle over me. One call rang through, unanswered. Another went straight to voicemail. A text message went unread. With each passing moment, the silence around us seemed louder, more pronounced.

I double-checked my email inbox, group messages, reminders sent earlier in the week, grasping for any small oversight I might have missed. But the information was correct, the messages clear, the communication thorough. Everything had been triple-checked. Everyone had confirmed.

As minutes turned into a quarter-hour, the student beside me seemed to understand what I was reluctant to admit: no one else was coming. He shifted quietly, looking at his shoes, the ground, anywhere but at me. I finally said aloud what we both knew: "Let's give them a few more minutes. Maybe someone got the wrong spot or time. Maybe someone's parking now." He nodded, but neither of us truly believed it.

When twenty minutes had passed without another arrival, I let out a gentle sigh. I finally said quietly, "I think we need to call it off." He nodded again, this time visibly disappointed. I assured him it wasn't his fault, thanked him for coming, and apologized for what had happened. As he walked away, backpack still slung loosely over his shoulder, he seemed smaller, somehow. I wondered what story he'd tell himself about today. Would he blame me,

INTRODUCTION

himself, his classmates? Would he remember this moment when another invitation came in the future?

I slowly unpacked the van. The water bottles, untouched, returned to storage. The journals and prayer guides were stacked neatly, waiting again for another day. Name tags slipped back into a folder, saved for the next retreat—if there was one. Each item carried a quiet disappointment, symbols of effort and expectation left unfulfilled.

Walking back toward my office afterward, the sun still shining incongruously bright, I felt the retreat's weight settling deeply within me. It wasn't simply logistical disappointment. It was personal. Spiritual. It whispered quietly about the nature of ministry itself—the hidden labor, the persistent hope, the painful letdowns. It was a reminder that sometimes ministry doesn't match our effort, no matter how sincere.

By the next morning, I had regained my public face. The one I used for hallway conversations and meetings. The one that explained away ministry mishaps with professional detachment. "Something came up, and we had to reschedule," I said with practiced ease to anyone who asked. It was not untrue—but neither was it the honest story. Beneath the professional veneer, a deeper silence remained unspoken. The true story of effort and disappointment, invisible yet heavy.

No one asked further. No one sought clarity or offered comfort. They accepted the explanation at face value, and we moved on quickly, neatly covering yesterday's failure in the routine of the present. When the retreat collapsed, that quiet effort collapsed with it—without recognition or acknowledgment.

Later that day, alone in my office, I kept returning to one persistent question: What more could I have done? The truthful answer? Nothing. Every step had been taken, every effort made. It had already been rescheduled once due to wildfires near the retreat center. Dates were chosen carefully, communication was thorough. Reminders were timely, follow-ups attentive. Integrity and effort had defined every step. Still, it was not enough. And perhaps the hardest realization: no one seemed to care why.

Part I: What We've Inherited

I gathered my belongings slowly, preparing to go home. The building was empty, hallways darkened, silence echoing. Yet in that quiet emptiness, one thought lingered clearly: Sometimes, you do everything right, and it still doesn't work. Not because your effort was lacking—but because ministry itself rests upon something more fragile, more complicated than we often admit. Something we've inherited but never quite acknowledged. Something silently breaking beneath us.

And yet that unnamed grief, that weight—those quiet resignations before every retreat, every liturgy, every unmet benchmark—those are not outside the Church. They are precisely what *Gaudium et Spes* names when it says, "The joys and the hopes, the griefs and the anxieties of the men of this age, especially those who are poor or in any way afflicted, these are the joys and hopes, the griefs and anxieties of the followers of Christ."[1] We are the baptized carrying the tension of hope in a Church that feels, some days, too tired to hope.

INVISIBLE EFFORT

What most people didn't see—what they rarely ever see—was the effort behind those seven names. Ministry is often a tapestry of quiet labors, woven together in obscurity. We're trained to value visibility, measurable outcomes, and tangible successes. But the true work of ministry often happens quietly, privately, away from view.

In the weeks leading up to the retreat, I visited multiple classrooms. Each visit required preparation and courage—to step into a space where I was interrupting a lesson, gently asking a teacher's permission to take a moment, and feeling dozens of teenage eyes turn my way, some curious, many indifferent. I shared briefly, inviting them into an experience they might otherwise overlook.

Then there were the personal invitations—quiet conversations in hallways, at lunch tables, after Mass. Each conversation

---

1. *Gaudium et Spes* §33

Introduction

was crafted, intentional, and hopeful. I remembered students' names, their interests, their struggles. I chose carefully whom I approached, thinking through their stories, what might draw them closer to an encounter. "I'd really love if you came," I'd say earnestly, often receiving a cautious "maybe" or a quiet, noncommittal shrug in response.

I wrote emails to parents, careful to craft each message warmly yet professionally, knowing their influence was essential. I outlined retreat details, benefits, and reassurance about safety and structure. Most parents never replied; the ones who did offered brief, polite affirmations or apologies.

All of this effort—invitations, emails, conversations—was more than logistical. It was emotional, spiritual, deeply personal. Each name was a seed planted with hope. Each confirmation felt like a tiny victory. Each silence or hesitation felt like a gentle setback.

These aren't the tasks you write about in annual reports. But they are ministry. And the Church has language for this. As *Christifideles Laici* reminds us, "Therefore, to respond to their vocation, the lay faithful must see their daily activities as an occasion to join themselves to God, fulfill his will, serve other people and lead them to communion with God in Christ."[2] Nothing we do—no spreadsheet, no folding chair, no broken conversation with a half-interested teenager—is wasted when it's carried in the name of Christ.

When the retreat collapsed, that invisible labor collapsed too—unacknowledged and unseen. No one witnessed the quiet grief of dismantling plans carefully laid, names carefully chosen, hopes carefully tended. Ministry is a quiet vocation—often invisible in success, painfully visible in failure. It asks that we hold these moments gently, even when no one else sees their weight. "We have this treasure in clay jars," Paul reminds us, "so that it may be made clear that this extraordinary power belongs to God and does not come from us."[3] The hardest part isn't always the lack of results.

---

2. *Christifideles Laici* §17
3. 2 Corinthians 4:7–9

Part I: What We've Inherited

Sometimes it's the silence that follows—when no one asks why, or what might be done differently.

THE STRUCTURAL MISMATCH

Sometimes, ministry events don't fail because of insufficient effort, poor preparation, or even lack of vision. Often, the true cause lies deeper, buried within the structure itself. The failure emerges quietly but inevitably, rooted in unexamined assumptions about what ministry should achieve and how it should look.

The retreat collapsed, not because the logistics failed or because the planning was poor, but because we were operating within expectations established in another era, another cultural moment—one long past. Institutional expectations had remained the same: gather students, lead them on retreat, produce meaningful spiritual outcomes, then move on quickly to the next event. Yet, the cultural, social, and spiritual realities had shifted dramatically beneath our feet. Students' schedules had grown busier, family priorities had shifted, and the rhythms of young people's spiritual lives had changed significantly. Ministry was still operating on a calendar, on a set of methods and goals, that no longer matched reality.

Administrators and supervisors asked for visible signs of success—high attendance, enthusiastic participation, photogenic moments of spiritual engagement—while quietly ignoring the increasingly strained soil in which we worked. They assumed participation would naturally happen, as it once had, with minimal relational groundwork. They presumed students would engage in faith experiences simply because they were offered, rather than because genuine trust had been built over time. Rather, they have told sociologists that they engage most in institutions, and by extension, feel engaged in the faith, when they feel like they belong through a process that Springtide Research Institute has called the Belongingness Process.[4]

---

4. Springside Research Institute. Belonging. P. 63.

INTRODUCTION

At meetings, I found myself explaining cultural shifts, declining birthrates in local parishes, dwindling youth participation, and changing family dynamics only to be met with blank stares or gentle skepticism. It felt like trying to plant seeds in cracked concrete, then being questioned about why nothing had sprouted.[5] No one paused to question the environment or acknowledge the shifting terrain beneath us.

Ministry was expected to happen, regardless of external changes. Institutional inertia demanded results without providing the necessary freedom, resources, or support to adjust methods, rethink assumptions, or redefine what success might mean in this new context. The result was not merely frustration, but deeper dissonance—feeling as if my integrity, sincerity, and effort were being measured against an outdated metric. Something vital was silently fracturing, not from lack of effort—but from assumptions no longer rooted in reality.

INHERITING BROKEN SYSTEMS

At a parish once, I stepped into a youth ministry role that had cycled rapidly through several staff members in just a few years. It was immediately apparent that I had inherited a system in quiet crisis. The students were cautious and detached, having seen adults come and go too many times. They had learned to shield themselves, to hold back from forming bonds that might abruptly break again. Each departure had subtly eroded trust, deepening a silent skepticism toward anyone new promising stability or meaning.

On my first day, I opened file cabinets filled with outdated paperwork, curriculum plans from years past, and carefully saved attendance sheets—names of students who no longer attended, no longer cared. On my desk sat a dusty binder labeled "Youth Ministry Resources," filled with icebreakers and retreat outlines that felt like relics of a different time. It quickly became clear that my job wasn't to simply engage students or provide meaningful formation.

5. Matthew 13:1–9

Part I: What We've Inherited

I was implicitly tasked with resurrecting a ministry program that had already lost its heartbeat long before I arrived.

I was told to report weekly attendance numbers to the pastor—an expectation that seemed almost absurd given the reality. Attendance implied active ministry, yet the group was nonexistent. I was pressured to produce immediate results with a program that held no presence, no compelling invitations, no relationships that might inspire attendance in the first place. Yet, there was little willingness from leadership to consider the deeper relational groundwork necessary to rebuild something genuine. The assumption was that a well-executed youth event—complete with colorful flyers, cheerful enthusiasm, and a charismatic leader—would magically draw students back, despite years of neglect.

Similarly, at a school once, I inherited a retreat and liturgy program rooted deeply in longstanding traditions and rituals, but practically devoid of communal responsibility or investment. The school calendar was impressively filled with liturgical events, reconciliation services, and multiple overnight retreats each year. Yet, the entirety of their planning and execution rested almost exclusively on one or two individuals. Events were expected to appear effortless, seamlessly integrated into school life, with minimal disruption to academics or athletics.

Evangelization is a process through which the evangelist accompanies the disaffiliating person. This process, known to sociologists as Relational Authority is the starting point for evangelization.[6] Without this foundation, the evangelist has no legs on which to stand.

The expectation was paradoxical: faith events were meant to feel profoundly meaningful and spiritually transformative but were supposed to demand no additional effort, support, or involvement from faculty. When these events succeeded, when students visibly engaged, it went largely unnoticed and was considered merely expected. Yet, when anything faltered—a scheduling conflict, a priest arriving late, a logistical hiccup—the fault fell squarely on the ministry coordinator's shoulders.

---

6. Springtide Research Institute, *Relational Authority*, 58, 74–97.

Introduction

Suggestions for improvement or innovation were often met with polite nods, acknowledgment, and occasional compliments about creativity or initiative. Yet tangible support rarely materialized. Ideas were heard but seldom acted upon. It became painfully clear that the institution did not actually desire meaningful, collaborative transformation; it simply wanted the appearance of spiritual vitality to remain undisturbed. Not because of any negativity in the administration or mission of the school, but rather it was something much deeper. Something in the very bones of the institution.

These experiences revealed something deeper and more troubling than mere lack of resources or occasional disinterest. They exposed inherited systems quietly buckling beneath unrealistic expectations, a chronic lack of support, and invisible relational labor never formally recognized or valued. Ministry was expected to function as if the structures beneath it were still healthy, vibrant, and relationally grounded, even as those structures silently eroded away beneath us.

When I arrived at each new ministry, I inherited a quiet burden alongside the practical responsibilities—a silent expectation that I would rebuild trust, renew enthusiasm, and revitalize community without acknowledgment of the relational damage[7] that had already occurred, the resources required to heal it, or the time necessary to build something authentically meaningful.

These were not isolated incidents. They were clear symptoms of deeper structural dysfunction—dysfunction I had inherited quietly, without formal training, conversation, or preparation. It became clear that the ministerial role wasn't merely to teach or inspire but often to quietly shoulder the impossible task of rebuilding and sustaining faith communities amidst deep, structural fractures that no one else seemed willing to acknowledge or address.

---

7. The scope of this work could not fit the extent of relational damage done by sexual or financial abuse scandals. However, those stories could fit in here likely even more appropriately than the constant professional turnover common to ministry roles.

Part I: What We've Inherited

THE WIDESPREAD NATURE OF THE PROBLEM

The more conversations I had with colleagues at diocesan gatherings, conferences, or informal meetings over coffee, the clearer it became that my experiences were far from unique. I began to hear echoes of familiar frustration and fatigue, not merely isolated complaints or occasional grievances, but consistent stories shared quietly by ministers who had similarly inherited fractured systems, unclear expectations, and declining institutional support.

At one diocesan event, I found myself in a corner speaking quietly with a youth minister whose vibrant enthusiasm visibly dimmed as she described the impossible pressures placed upon her to grow attendance, produce photographic evidence of student engagement, and build relational trust overnight, all without meaningful support or clear guidance from her pastor. Another colleague shared how their parish expected growth and vitality without ever acknowledging the practical reality that the number of young families in the community had steadily declined. Still another described how his principal repeatedly praised the value of retreats and liturgies publicly, yet privately provided almost no tangible support, leaving the minister isolated, quietly overwhelmed, and increasingly discouraged.

These moments weren't outliers—they formed a troubling pattern. The faces changed, the parishes or schools varied, but the underlying ache remained consistent. Ministry leaders across various settings and roles repeatedly shared a similar experience: being asked to accomplish more with fewer resources, less support, and no meaningful structural changes. Quiet conversations revealed a collective exhaustion—a fatigue born not simply from the physical or logistical demands of ministry, but from deeper emotional and spiritual exhaustion that comes from feeling persistently unseen, unheard, and undervalued.

The problems we faced were not personal failures or isolated circumstances. They were systemic, quietly affecting nearly every lay minister I spoke to. The shared experiences pointed to something deeper: an inherited structure quietly fracturing, demanding

INTRODUCTION

impossible outcomes without acknowledging the quiet labor and relational foundations necessary for authentic spiritual growth.

THE PERFORMANCE MACHINE

Increasingly, ministry has become synonymous with measurable outcomes. Administrators, pastors, and parish councils have subtly shifted their definition of success from quiet transformation and deepening relationships to immediately recognizable, visibly appealing results. In a world trained to notice the large, the loud, and the impressive, it's easy to miss the spiritual weight of the silent faith. Christ didn't. He saw the widow's two coins for what they were: everything she had.[8] In ministry, the most faithful acts are often equally invisible—seen only by the One who knows the cost. We have entered a new era in which optics overshadow authenticity, and appearance becomes more important than substance. Quiet spiritual growth and gradual formation have become secondary within a performance-based ministry model.

In this landscape, ministers often feel less like pastoral companions and more like brand managers. They are subtly pressured to create visible, shareable moments—photos of smiling students holding Bibles, packed retreats looking vibrant, staged scenes of prayerful reflection that project spiritual success. The expectation is clear: if ministry appears active and engaging, then it must be spiritually effective.

Social media posts become markers of success, creating an insidious pressure to present faith as perpetually joyful, effortlessly vibrant, and consistently successful. Ministers find themselves capturing images during liturgies, retreats, or prayer services—not to document genuine spiritual breakthroughs, but simply to produce proof of engagement. Every event must be photogenic, every moment potentially shareable, every result easily quantifiable.

This shift creates quiet tension. On one hand, ministers genuinely desire vibrant, meaningful spiritual experiences. On

---

8. Luke 21:1–4

the other hand, the pressure to produce performative spirituality undermines genuine relationship-building. Ministry becomes transactional, event-based, superficial. Quiet, transformative conversations—ones that truly shape hearts—become less valued simply because they're harder to document, less obvious to outside observers. Authentic spiritual formation is rarely photogenic, seldom immediate, and often messy—traits incompatible with a culture demanding instant results and appealing visuals.

The performance machine quietly demands more. More attendance. More events. More visibly happy participants. Yet, it rarely pauses to ask deeper, harder questions: Are hearts genuinely transformed? Do these events foster meaningful discipleship? Do students or parishioners carry faith meaningfully beyond these moments?

In fact, the pressure to maintain optics often obscures underlying spiritual realities. We might have fifty smiling students captured in a well-lit Instagram post, yet few genuine conversations about their doubts, struggles, or spiritual questions. A parish event might appear vibrant and thriving, yet few realize attendance relied entirely upon obligatory participation, superficial incentives, or carefully managed appearances.

And what happens when the optics falter? The retreat with low attendance, the Mass sparsely attended, the event without shareable photographs? Instead of prompting thoughtful reflection about deeper spiritual needs or systemic challenges, institutional response is often simply: "Try harder." Not "Try differently." Not "Let's re-evaluate expectations." Simply harder.

This performative approach quietly erodes genuine ministry. Ministers become marketers, constantly anxious about optics rather than genuinely invested in quiet, relational discipleship. The underlying assumption—that vibrant spirituality can be mass-produced and visibly packaged—is quietly, dangerously flawed.

When the goal becomes appearance rather than authenticity, optics rather than outcomes, ministry ceases to genuinely form disciples. Instead, it quietly forms exhausted ministers, disillusioned parishioners, and disaffected students—those quietly

Introduction

stepping away from faith because the performative machine never truly met them where they were.

I recognize that the book so far can come off as critical. But I want to be clear: I don't believe this pressure is the fault of any one person. No one designed the machine, and few would claim to run it. Most pastors and administrators I've known genuinely care about the souls entrusted to them. They don't wake up in the morning scheming to measure grace in likes, attendance logs, or high-energy photos. But the metrics are baked in. Budgets, staff reviews, parish council meetings, and diocesan reports all bend toward the visible. The machine doesn't need a driver—it just needs momentum. And once it's moving, even faithful leaders can be swept along by its logic. Stopping to ask whether this is actually forming anyone can feel, ironically, like derailing the very mission we set out to serve.

Still, I believe ministry within this system is no less sacred. To labor in its shadow with honesty and hope—to serve without spotlight, to love without applause—is a quiet kind of holiness.

I know this section, and some of the rest of the book may read, at times, as more venting than vision. I've wondered that myself while writing it. But the emotional texture matters. Ministry isn't abstract—it's personal. If the voice occasionally sounds tired or strained, it's because ministry often is. I'm not writing from the outside looking in. I'm writing from inside the weight of it. And if that weight shows through, it's only because I'm still carrying it. So are you, probably.

BURNOUT BENEATH THE SURFACE

We often imagine burnout as a dramatic moment: the resignation letter, the tearful goodbye, the minister who finally walks away. But in reality, burnout is usually quiet. It happens slowly, accumulating like dust in the corners of a heart that once held fire. Most burned-out ministers are still showing up, still organizing, still smiling in photos. But inside, something essential has dulled.

Part I: What We've Inherited

Burnout is not just physical exhaustion or mental fatigue. It's a spiritual condition. It emerges when the soul begins to separate from the work it once embraced as vocation. When hope feels like naivety. When the idealism that brought you into ministry is replaced by low-grade cynicism masked as realism. You stop expecting things to change. You stop believing anyone will listen. You begin doing only what is necessary to keep the machine running, because dreaming beyond that has become too painful.

One of the most dangerous things about ministry burnout is that it rarely triggers concern. Instead, it often looks like quiet compliance. You stop asking difficult questions. You let poor decisions pass without comment. You lower your expectations—not out of laziness, but as a form of self-protection. You become a master of accommodation, not because you're at peace, but because you know the cost of confrontation is too high and the payoff too low. You say yes when you want to say no. You stay silent when something in you wants to scream.

This kind of burnout doesn't happen because someone lacks faith. It happens because someone believed deeply—so deeply that the repeated collisions with indifference, apathy, or institutional rigidity finally became too much. Burnout happens not in the absence of care, but because of care that was repeatedly offered and rarely returned.

And the most insidious part? Ministry often rewards it. A burned-out minister can still plan events. They can still run retreats, manage volunteers, and give talks that sound sincere. Because they know the rhythms so well, they can keep the machine humming even while their spirit is running on fumes. The performance might not falter, but the person behind it is quietly fading.

We don't just burn out from doing too much. We burn out from doing too much that doesn't matter. From giving hours to meetings that never produce change. From planning events that no one attends. From pouring ourselves out in spaces where we are barely noticed. Burnout is not just depletion—it is depletion without meaning.

Introduction

And most hauntingly, burnout can look like holiness. Quiet suffering. Tireless service. Self-denial. These are virtues in the Christian imagination, and rightly so. But when they become masks for despair, when they serve to hide rather than heal, they stop being virtues and start becoming wounds. Holy-looking burnout is still burnout.

What would it take for our institutions to recognize this? What if the real danger wasn't ministers who finally leave—but those who stay, numbed and unseen, doing just enough to keep the illusion alive? What if our crisis isn't merely a lack of vocations, but a quiet exodus happening inside the walls? Burnout is not a personal failure. It is a communal warning. It tells the truth about our systems before anyone dares to speak it aloud.

THE THEOLOGICAL COST

Ministry burnout is not just psychological wear—it's a theological crisis. When you spend enough time in environments where visibility replaces transformation, where metrics are mistaken for mission, and where effort is valued only if it yields numbers, your understanding of God can begin to warp. Slowly, subtly, you trade the burning bush for the golden calf.

You say God cares about the lost and the least—but your day is spent building up programs that keep the already-involved happy. You say the Spirit moves in silence and mystery—but your work is measured in photos, attendance sheets, and bullet points for the report. You say Christ meets us in weakness—but your job requires you to always look strong. And when that contradiction becomes normal, it begins to do violence to your soul.

This is the slow spiritual disfigurement that institutional ministry often causes. Not because the people are cruel, or the intentions bad—but because the logic of the system does not always match the logic of the Gospel. The system wants clarity, predictability, and results. The Gospel calls for trust, sacrifice, and unmeasurable love. When those come into conflict, you are asked—implicitly or explicitly—to serve the system. And you do.

Because you care. Because it's your job. Because it's your vocation. But each time you compromise your deepest convictions for institutional survival, something sacred gets harder to find.

You begin to wonder: do I still believe the things I teach? Not abstractly—of course you believe them. But do you believe them in your bones, in the lived reality of your ministry? Do you believe that grace is enough, when your budget isn't? That the Spirit leads, when your calendar is already full? That Christ builds the Church, when it feels like it's falling apart on your watch? These questions are not signs of weak faith. They are signs of a minister trying to hold faith in a system that often undermines it.

We do not name this cost often enough. We assume the theological weight is something we can carry quietly, that prayer and perseverance will patch over the gaps. But this isn't just about needing more self-care or better boundaries. It's about needing better theology—one that sees the minister not as a tool of the institution but as a person within the Body, deserving of grace, accompaniment, and rest.[9]

The Gospel is not an institutional strategy. It is the living story of God's love poured out in weakness, in slowness, in what the world would call foolish hope. If our ministry structures cannot reflect that, then no amount of good intentions will save them. The cost is not just ours. It is born by the people who never meet the God we say we represent—because we ourselves are struggling to see Him in our own work.

The theological cost is not that we stop believing. It's that we begin to believe something smaller.

WHAT YOUNG PEOPLE ARE REALLY LEAVING

We talk about disaffiliation like it's a rebellion. We tally up the statistics, run the exit interviews, and speak of "those who left" as if they've abandoned something self-evidently good. But most of

---

9. 1 Corinthians 12:12–27

Introduction

the time, they didn't leave the Church in a dramatic act of protest. When in reality, the story is much different.

The Center for Applied Research in the Apostolate and St. Mary's Press released a study that changed the entire landscape of ministry with disaffiliating Catholics. This study, Going, Going, Gone: The Dynamics of Disaffiliation in Young Catholics is a qualitative rather than quantitative study. This is key because the qualitative study allowed for the voices of the young people to finally break through the loud silence. In this work, the sociologists described three categories of people who left the Church: the injured, the drifters, and the dissenters.[10]

They just stopped coming. Quietly. Slowly. They slipped out through the side door while we were tweaking the welcome message on the front steps. They're not fleeing the Gospel. They're backing away from a version of Church life that never made space for them to speak, lead, or be taken seriously.

Some of them were never even seen. These may be called the drifters. They came to youth nights and found no one their age. They sat through confirmation classes that felt like chores, not calls. They tried to ask hard questions and were met with canned answers or polite redirection. They showed up with longing and were handed a clipboard. And over time, they learned what many of us already knew: participation isn't the same as belonging. And belonging isn't the same as mattering.

They are not walking away from Christ. They are walking away from a system that could not imagine them as more than a passive audience. What we call "disaffiliation" is often just the end of a one-sided relationship. They showed up. They waited to be noticed. They waited to be needed. And eventually, they stopped waiting.

And yet, we keep diagnosing the problem in terms of catechesis, doctrine, discipline. We act as though better arguments will bring them back. We double down on programs that didn't work the first time. We repackage the same formation strategies with a new logo. And we're confused when it doesn't land.

---

10. Saint Mary's Press, *Going, Going, Gone*, 13–31.

But if you listen closely—really listen—you'll hear that most young people are not asking, "Is the Church true?" They're asking, "Is the Church real?" Real enough to see me. Real enough to trust me. They are not waiting to be entertained. They are waiting to be known.

This is the central failure: we kept offering young people a place to sit when what they needed was a place to stand. And now, we're surprised they've moved on.

We will not rebuild trust by demanding loyalty. We will not call them back by guilt or fear or clever branding. We will only draw them if we become something worth coming back to—if we are honest about our failings, bold about our hopes, and willing to give away real ownership, not just participation.

They are not rejecting holiness. They are rejecting irrelevance. They are not anti-sacramental. They are anti-fake. And they are watching us carefully—not to see how cool we've become, but to see if we're serious enough to let go of control.

What they are leaving is not faith. It's the illusion of belonging without investment. What they need is not an invitation to come back. It's a reason to believe they were ever truly wanted in the first place.

GRACE BREAKS THROUGH

And yet—grace breaks through. Not in the headlines. Not in the strategic plans. Not in the metrics we're asked to submit. But in the quiet places we almost forget to look.

I have seen a student go from indifference to tears during a retreat talk—not because the talk was especially profound, but because it named something real in his life for the first time. I have seen a student stay after Mass to ask a question that had been weighing on him for months. I have seen young leaders take ownership of a retreat moment, not because they were told to, but because the Spirit stirred something in them that couldn't be ignored.

Introduction

These aren't marketing moments. They don't translate well to social media or staff reports. They are glimpses of something deeper—proof that the Spirit is still moving, even when the institution is creaking under its own weight.

Grace does not need our systems to function perfectly. It often works in spite of them, in spite of ourselves. In the cracks and gaps, in the missed connections and awkward silences, grace finds a way. Springtide Research calls this landscape Relational Authority. These awkward silences, painful moments, walking together starts with this relational authority.[11] It doesn't erase the difficulty. It doesn't undo the disappointment. But it makes the struggle matter.

These moments are why many of us stay. Not out of obligation or habit, but because somewhere along the way, we caught a glimpse of the real thing. And that glimpse was enough to keep going.

Some still care. Some still show up. Some still pray with longing, serve with love, and ask their hard, honest questions. And that should be enough to make us pause. To reexamine everything we've built. To ask whether the systems we've inherited are worthy of the hunger we still see in the hearts of those who haven't walked away.

WHAT THIS BOOK IS (AND ISN'T)

This book is not a manual. It is not a strategy guide, a marketing plan, or a toolkit for boosting numbers. It is not a repackaging of old answers with updated fonts. It is not a spiritual pep talk dressed in pastoral platitudes. And it is certainly not a how-to for managing the optics of ministry more effectively.

I'm not going to give you ten ways to get students back to Mass. I'm not going to rebrand discipleship to sound more exciting or make evangelization feel like recruitment. I'm not going to pretend that ministry is easy, or that better graphics will solve what broken trust has eroded.

I will name what we've inherited—both the treasures and the burdens. I will give voice to the exhaustion that too many of us

---

11. Springtide Research Institute, *Relational Authority*, 74–97.

have learned to carry in silence. I will honor the work we've done, the moments of grace we've witnessed, and the questions we can no longer ignore.

This is not a book about giving up. It is a book about staying—with integrity. I'm not writing this as a theologian with a solution or a director with a plan. I'm writing this as someone who has stayed—sometimes resentfully, sometimes barely. And that, too, is witness. As *Evangelii Nuntiandi* puts it, "Modern man listens more willingly to witnesses than to teachers. . . and if he does listen to teachers, it is because they are first witnesses."[12] I'm not interested in theorizing about ministry. I'm writing from the inside of it—exhausted, invested, and still believing it matters.

Finally, it's a book meant to walk alongside you. At the end of each part, you'll find Accompaniment Meditations. The meditations are moments to pause, to breathe, to reflect on your own call and burnout and belonging. These interludes are not decoration. They are part of the testimony. Because some of us are still here. Still showing up. Still hoping. Still praying that something deeper can emerge—not in spite of the disaffiliation we're witnessing, but through it.

We don't need new gimmicks. We need new imagination. We need the courage to ask whether what we're building is worth the weight it places on the people tasked with holding it together.

If you're reading this, you're probably one of those people.

This book is for you.

---

12. *Evangelii Nuntiandi* §41

Chapter 1

Ministry Without Authority

THE WEIGHT WITHOUT THE VOICE

THERE IS A PARTICULAR kind of exhaustion that sets in when you are held accountable for something you are not empowered to shape. It's not the fatigue of hard work—most lay ministers are no strangers to long days or emotional labor. It's something different. It's the spiritual toll of carrying responsibility without authority, of being asked to produce results from systems you don't control.

We are often tasked with big goals: revive the retreat program, increase attendance, make the liturgies more engaging, help students or parishioners feel spiritually invested. The mission is clear. The outcomes are expected. But when we look around to ask how we're supposed to get there—what resources we have, what collaboration we can count on, what flexibility we're allowed—it becomes evident that the real decisions are made elsewhere. Yet our shepherds have called lay ecclesial ministry something entirely different. This, "ecclesial service is characterized by:

- Authorization of the hierarchy to serve publicly in the local church
- Leadership in a particular area of ministry

Part I: What We've Inherited

- Close mutual collaboration with the pastoral ministry of priests, bishops, and deacons
- Preparation and formation appropriate to the level of responsibilities that are assigned to them"[1]

In the Directory for Catechesis, the Pontifical Council for the Promotion of the New Evangelization puts it more succinctly. Here they say that, catechists are witnesses to the faith, teachers, and companions.[2]

In many schools and parishes, the minister's job is defined not by a shared vision but by inherited expectations. Events happen because they've always happened. Programs continue because someone put them on the calendar years ago. And when they falter, the blame rarely travels upward. The lay minister becomes both the face and the fallback: accountable for everything, consulted about very little.

This is not a complaint about oversight. Accountability is important. We are stewards of the people we serve, and we should be answerable for our work. The problem arises when the expectations are mismatched with the authority. When you are responsible for creating spiritual depth in a community but not allowed to restructure the schedule to make space for it. When you are expected to grow attendance but not permitted to investigate why people aren't coming. When you are charged with forming hearts but can't choose the tools to do it.

At its core, this disconnect reveals a deeper ecclesial tension: the Church has leaned heavily on lay ministers to keep things going—but has not always adapted its internal culture to support them. In many settings, authority remains clerical, hierarchical, and cautious. Don't mistake this challenge: this is not advocacy for fully horizontal decision making. The synodality that Pope Francis called for is not laicization of authority, but rather a recognition that there are certain skills that pastors lack, the acknowledgement that their calendar will not allow them to be in two places at once.

---

1. USCCB, *Co-Workers in the Vineyard*, 10.
2. *Directory for Catechesis*, §113

MINISTRY WITHOUT AUTHORITY

Yet under this current framework, creativity is tolerated, not cultivated. Innovation is suspect. And suggestions from those without collars or titles are often met with polite deflection.

The emotional cost of this becomes hard to name. You start to second-guess your instincts. You begin shrinking your ideas to fit what's been "approved" before. You learn not to push too hard, because the pushback isn't worth it. And when something does succeed, you're quietly aware that it worked in spite of the structure, not because of it. The Church herself recognizes this fact, "how great a distance lies between the message she offers and the human failings of those to whom the Gospel is entrusted."[3]

Still, you stay. Not because it's easy, but because you believe in the mission. You believe that grace works through small cracks. You believe that presence matters, even when the system feels immovable. And you believe that somehow, this weight you carry—this tension of responsibility without voice—is still worth holding, because the people you serve are worth it.

But if we're serious about forming disciples and not just maintaining appearances, then this structure has to be named. Ministry cannot thrive when it is led from the margins without a path toward real influence. The mission of evangelization belongs to the whole Church—and so must the discernment and decisions that shape how we pursue it.

INVITATIONS WITHOUT ACCESS

In many parishes and schools, the language of collaboration is strong. Lay ministers are often told they are part of the team, or integral to the mission. And to some extent, these things are true. We are invited to planning meetings. We receive the agendas. We sit in the rooms. But presence is not the same as participation. And being welcome is not the same as being trusted.

There's a kind of invitation that flatters without empowering. You are asked for input—but only after the decisions have already

---

3. *Gaudium et Spes* §43

been made. You are told your insight is valuable—but only if it affirms the direction already chosen. You are included—but with the unspoken expectation that your role is to carry out, not to question.

Over time, you learn the difference between speaking and shaping. You can voice your opinion, as long as it doesn't disrupt the flow. You can make a suggestion, as long as it doesn't require institutional change. And you can offer feedback, as long as you're prepared for it to be politely ignored.

This kind of pseudo-access is disorienting. On paper, it looks like inclusion. In practice, it feels like performance. You are invited in, but the deeper message is clear: you're here to help execute—not to lead. Your presence is meant to give the appearance of collaboration, not the reality of shared discernment.

I once attended a series of liturgical planning meetings that illustrated this perfectly. The schedule was already set. The themes had been chosen. The major decisions had been finalized. The team was gathered to collaborate, but it became quickly obvious that the goal was logistical distribution—not visioning. An important task, but nowhere near the heart of the conversation I had thought I was being invited into.

This is not unique. Many lay ministers find themselves constantly delegated to—their time, their energy, their presence—without ever being asked what they see from the ground. The assumption is that ministry is the execution of someone else's vision. That the best contribution a lay minister can make is to say yes quickly and carry it through.

But vision is where mission begins. And when those who carry the weight of ministry are excluded from the shaping of it, something essential is lost. The Church begins to speak with only part of its voice.

To be clear, most pastors and leaders don't intend this dynamic. They believe they are being inclusive, synodal even. They are grateful for your help. But structural dynamics don't require bad intentions to have real consequences. When the table is set and the meal already cooked, being invited to sit down doesn't mean you had a hand in what's being served.

If we truly believe in the co-responsibility of the baptized, then invitations into leadership must carry the weight of agency. Otherwise, we are simply dressing up old hierarchies in the language of collaboration.

EXPECTATIONS WITHOUT AUTHORITY

One of the great contradictions of lay ministry is the disconnect between expectations and authority. We are expected to animate tired programs, increase student engagement, organize meaningful liturgies, and coordinate impactful retreats—all with limited time, limited resources, and even more limited decision-making power. The bar for excellence is high. The tools to attain it are often out of reach.

We are not asked to keep the lights on. We are asked to breathe new life into old frameworks. To make the retreat "more meaningful," the service hour program "more transformative." And yet, we rarely have control over the elements that define success. We inherit calendars we didn't plan, venues we didn't choose, and expectations we didn't help shape. The outcome is ours to own, but the structure that produces it is not ours to adjust.

This creates a kind of invisible tension. When something works well, it's business as usual. When something falters, the question quietly turns toward us. Why weren't there more sign-ups? Why wasn't that liturgy smoother? Why didn't parents get more involved? The implication is that we are responsible for the fruit, regardless of the soil.

At one school, I was tasked with coordinating a weekend liturgy meant to serve as a celebration of our patron saint. It was placed on a Saturday. Everyone on the planning team knew the turnout would be low—weekend events had always suffered from poor attendance—but the expectation remained: plan something beautiful, and make it feel full. I did everything I could. I promoted the Mass, extended personal invitations, worked with our student leaders, even reached out to alumni. When the day came, no students arrived. Not one. We ended up pulling in a family working on their Eagle Scout project just to ensure that someone was present who wasn't paid to be there.

There was no postmortem, no discussion about how to improve future participation. The failure wasn't named aloud, but it hung in the air—heavy and unspoken. Once again, the event had been expected to succeed. Once again, it hadn't. And once again, no one asked what structural support might be needed to make it work differently next time.

This dynamic isn't limited to events. It extends to curriculum, communication, and collaboration to name a few. We are held accountable for the results of systems we did not design, but we are not given the authority to adjust them. We are expected to carry the mission, but not to clarify its methods.

And in that gap—between what we're asked to do and what we're allowed to influence—morale begins to erode. Not because we don't love the work, but because the work is often set up to quietly wear us down. Responsibility without authority is not stewardship. It's slow erosion dressed up as leadership.

MINISTRY BY DEFAULT

There is a subtle but pervasive reality in lay ministry: much of what we do is not strategically assigned, but rather silently absorbed. Responsibilities trickle down, not because they align with our strengths or mission, but because no one else is doing them. This is ministry by default—carrying what has been dropped, covering what has been neglected, and continuing programs that do not or no longer have champions but still appear on the calendar.

At one parish, I was regularly asked to coordinate students to take up second collections during Sunday Mass—not for any theological or formational reason, but simply because the business manager thought it looked good to have youth involvement. The implication was clear: it didn't matter whether students understood what they were doing or why. It mattered that they were visible enough to be noticed, enough to check the optics box.

In another setting, I found myself responsible for livestreaming Masses during the pandemic. I had no training in AV production, no support team, and no additional pay—but I was the youngest person on staff, and therefore assumed to be the most tech-savvy. The rationale was as straightforward as it was frustrating: "You're the millennial. You'll figure it out." I did. But it came at the cost of energy, time, and bandwidth that should have gone toward pastoral care and formation.

These are not horror stories. They are the norm. In schools, lay ministers take on spiritual programming not because it is prioritized, but because no one else has the time. In parishes, we inherit registration systems, lesson plans, and calendar rhythms from a past we didn't shape, and are expected to execute them flawlessly. Faith formation, parent communication, sacramental prep, student engagement—it all lands in our inbox, because although we are the best and most equipped to handle it, often the additional reason is because the original owner of the responsibility has moved on, burnt out, or opted out.

No one stops to question how sustainable this is. But imagine if they did. Imagine a parish where sustainability wasn't a crisis to be solved after burnout, but a value baked into the culture from the start. Where ministry wasn't absorbed by the most willing person, but distributed wisely among a community that understood shared mission. Where pastors didn't just delegate, but collaborated. Where lay ministers weren't constantly compensating for absence, but building from presence.

Imagine a parish staff that prays together—not performatively, not as a five-minute add-on before the agenda, but because they believe grace is necessary to do this well. A community that celebrates rest as much as output. That tracks stories of transformation, not just sacrament tallies. Where parents volunteer not because they're guilted into it, but because they've been personally invited, formed, and trusted. Where ministers are known by name, not job title. Where someone notices when you're tired and says,

"You can sit this one out. We've got you." It wouldn't be perfect. But it would be real. And it would be enough to remind us that this work doesn't have to hollow us out. That ministry can be shared, gentle, and whole.

Instead, too often, there's a difference between stepping into a role and standing in for someone else indefinitely. One is a call; the other is slow substitution. When clergy are overburdened, families are disengaged, or leadership is inattentive, lay ministers become the stopgap. We are expected to be the bridge, the glue, the back-up plan. And while most of us do this gladly, the cost adds up. Especially when no one acknowledges that we're carrying more than we were meant to hold.

Ministry becomes not the joyful response to a call, but the steady accumulation of inherited tasks. What was once rooted in mission starts to feel like a mop-up job for institutional neglect.

A DIFFERENT KIND OF LEADERSHIP

If we are not clergy, not administrators, and not decision-makers, then what kind of leaders are we? This question surfaces often—sometimes in frustration, sometimes in quiet reflection—among those of us who carry the daily weight of ministry without the formal structures of authority. We are responsible for forming hearts, mentoring souls, and carrying forward the mission of the Church. Yet we often do so from the edges of the decision-making circle. The challenge is not only practical, but theological: what does leadership look like when it has no formal power?

The answer is not resignation. It is redefinition.

True leadership in ministry is not about holding the highest title. It's about carrying the deepest fidelity. Lay ministers lead not because they are in charge, but because they are rooted. Rooted in presence. Rooted in listening. Rooted in an unshakable commitment to keep showing up, even when the structures falter. We may not have a vote at the table, but we have a voice. And when that voice speaks from prayer, integrity, and lived witness, it carries its own kind of authority.

This is spiritual authority—not conferred by a job title, but earned through consistency, compassion, and credibility. It's the kind of authority that comes from knowing your students by name, to walking with them through heartbreak not because it's your job, but because it's your vocation. It's not the authority to direct an institution. It's the authority to shepherd a heart.

In a world where leadership is often conflated with power, budgets, and visibility, lay ministers model something else: leadership by presence. We become trustworthy not because we're flashy, but because we're faithful.

This is exactly what our disaffiliating generation is watching. They are not seeking the most polished event or the best merch. They are looking for people who live the Gospel with enough credibility to take seriously.[4] They are listening for leaders who don't just talk about prayer, but who live lives marked by prayer. They want witnesses, not just speakers. They want relationship, not just role models. They want someone who can carry the weight of spiritual questions without defaulting to slogans or strategies.

Leadership in this context is not performative. It's sacrificial. It's not about making decisions that shape an institution. It's about making choices that reflect Christ. We must keep naming the structures that need reform and keep asking for the support that ministry deserves. But while we wait for that change we must also reclaim what it means to lead.

That means leading with integrity when no one is watching. It means mentoring others without needing credit. It means investing in students, parents, or volunteers even when the metrics don't show it. It means staying close to Christ so that our leadership remains more than just programming. Because when all the systems fall short—and they often do—it is that kind of leadership that holds.

Ministry without authority doesn't mean ministry without power. It just means our power takes a different form: the form of presence, prayer, and prophetic witness. The form of the Cross.

---

4. Springtide Research Institute, *Relational Authority*, 92–97.

Chapter 2

The Optics of Engagement

COUNTING WHAT CAN BE SEEN

How many students attended the retreat? How many service hours were completed? How many kids showed up to youth group this week compared to last? These are the questions that fill ministry reports, administrative meetings, and annual evaluations. They are the data points requested by principals, pastors, diocesan officials, and sometimes even parents. On their own, they aren't malicious. Numbers have their place. But over time, the gravitational pull toward what can be counted begins to reshape what is actually prioritized.

Ministry becomes a numbers game—not because ministers want it to be, but because the culture demands it. And so, we begin collecting. We count heads at Mass, sign-ups for sacraments, RSVPs for service projects. We track attendance at adoration nights and monitor retreat rosters for upward trends. If something doesn't yield visible fruit, we worry it will be perceived as ineffective. We preempt criticism by front-loading our work with quantifiable wins. We lead with the optics—what looks full, what looks joyful, what looks successful. There is nothing wrong with photos of joyful ministry. We want joy. But when photos become proof of vitality, rather than expressions of it, something starts to unravel.

The Optics of Engagement

There is a subtle shift in how we evaluate our work. Quiet conversations with students no longer seem like a worthwhile use of time, unless they can be translated into testimonial quotes. Unseen moments of consolation or repentance become less meaningful unless they lead to a shareable story. A beautifully simple liturgy, reverent and prayerful, may be judged less favorably than a loud praise night that fills the gym. And once that shift happens—once what we count becomes what we value—we begin to shape ministry around the report rather than the relationship. This isn't just an aesthetic problem. It's a theological one. Pope Francis called all into the art of accompaniment: priests, religious and laity.[1]

We are asked to deliver transformation, but measured by participation. We are asked to form disciples, but are evaluated by engagement. The assumption is that visible activity equals spiritual growth. But anyone who has worked in ministry for more than five minutes knows that some of the most profound transformations happen slowly, silently, and far from the spotlight. You don't always see the grace unfolding. You don't always get the closure of a conversion story.

Some of the most powerful work I've witnessed happened in moments that no photo could capture. A student staying after class to ask, in halting words, whether God could really forgive them. A retreatant slipping into adoration long after the event had ended. A senior showing up for confession, shaking but resolute, without anyone asking them to come. These are not the moments that show up in the slideshow. But they are the moments that matter.

Still, we are pressured to produce visibility. Social media accounts need new content. Newsletters need uplifting stories. School websites want banners of smiling students. It's not just the photos—it's the need for a narrative that sounds impressive. Something that can prove to a donor, a parent, or a board member that ministry is working. So, we make it look like it's working.

We lean into events that photograph well. We quote students who say the right things. We push for visible engagement, because visible engagement keeps us funded, respected, and safe from

---

1. *Evangelii Gaudium* §169

criticism. But what gets lost in this exchange is the slow work of the Spirit. The mustard seed moments. The movements of conscience that take years to flower. The tearful admissions that don't end in a picture-perfect resolution. Those are harder to quantify—but they're the real work of formation.

Until we recalibrate our measures of success, we will keep building ministries that look healthy but lack depth. We will keep exhausting ministers who feel the tension between what is needed and what is demanded. And we will keep losing young people who long for something real, but keep getting offered something staged. The Church doesn't need more optics. It needs more witnesses. And those are harder to count.

MARKETABLE MINISTRY OR REAL ENCOUNTER?

There is a growing expectation in ministry today that every moment must be brandable. Retreats must be vibrant. Liturgies must be aesthetic. Student reflections must sound like testimonial reels. Even prayer, if possible, should look good on camera. Ministry is not just asked to be meaningful—it's asked to be marketable. We are not just forming disciples. We are producing content.

At first, this pressure arrives subtly. A request to grab photos during the retreat. A reminder to post something engaging on the ministry page. A suggestion to highlight students who "really got something out of it." None of these are unreasonable on their own. It's good to show the life of the Church. But over time, these small pressures compound into something bigger: the assumption that if you didn't capture it, it didn't count.

Joy becomes performative. Students are nudged to write about what they got out of an event before they've even had time to reflect. Moments of grace are packaged into captions. The messier parts—the questions, the resistance, the silence—are left out because they don't make for good optics. The quiet student who didn't raise their hand, who didn't sing during praise and worship, who didn't cry at the retreat—they disappear from the story entirely, even if the Spirit was moving in them more deeply than anyone else.

Real formation is often slow, boring, and unshareable. It happens in repetition, in doubt, in awkward conversations that don't resolve neatly. But those don't trend. So instead, we spotlight the loudest moments and trim the rest. There is a cost to this.

Students can feel when something is being staged. They know when a camera is present for their reaction. They sense when their story is being used to sell a program. Even if they smile through it, it shapes how they show up in the future. They become more self-conscious. More filtered. Less likely to be real.

And ministers, in turn, begin to shape events around what will look good. We favor music that gets a visible response. We shorten talks so they don't lose the room. We craft moments that feel spiritual, but not too intense—something you can caption, but not something that requires accompaniment afterward. That's not evangelization. That's marketing. And it's exhausting.

Because real ministry—the kind that changes lives—isn't efficient or easy to brand. It requires presence, trust, and patience. It asks us to stay even when there's no story to post. It calls us to protect sacred moments from exploitation, even when someone asks for a photo.

There is nothing wrong with beauty. Nothing wrong with joy. But when those become performances for others rather than fruits of grace, we have lost the thread. "The Church has always had the task of scrutinizing the signs of the times and interpreting them in the light of the Gospel."[2] The Church doesn't need better PR. It needs better presence. Because real encounter is never marketable.

MINISTRY THAT RESISTS THE FRAME

The most important ministry moments never make it into the newsletter. They happen in quiet conversations on the edge of a fire pit. In the car ride after a hard confession. They unfold over

---

2. *Gaudium et Spes* §4

months, not hours, and they rarely lend themselves to clean summaries or compelling visuals. No one claps for them. No one asks for a recap. But these are the moments when transformation begins to take root.

The problem is that our institutional systems are built to notice only what fits in the frame. Success is measured in sacramental prep rosters, social media engagement, retreat attendance, and anecdotal wins that can be quoted in a grant application. Even well-meaning administrators need proof of life—and proof is easier to offer when it looks like a number or a photo.

But ministry doesn't move on that timeline. And formation rarely follows that script. A student who starts showing up for events after months of avoidance. A parent who re-engages quietly after years away. A colleague who begins to pray again—not loudly, but sincerely. These are signs of grace, not strategy. And they resist easy explanation.

The longer one remains in ministry, the more one notices this gap. The institution asks for the highlight reel. But the real work is hidden. Which is why it matters so deeply that we, as ministers, learn to name what we see—especially when no one else is looking. That moment when a student chooses service over popularity. That breakthrough when a resistant group finally opens up in small group prayer. That slow, hard walk alongside someone whose faith is barely flickering. These aren't just side notes. They are the story.

But they won't show up in the metrics. They won't trend. And they won't impress stakeholders who are looking for the immediate return. So we learn to tell the truth anyway. We learn to trust the unseen. To celebrate what doesn't get counted. To hold onto the belief that ministry has always been more like gardening than performance. It requires patience, presence, and a willingness to sow without certainty.

In doing so, we model something essential for the people we serve. We show them that God doesn't need their lives to be impressive—just faithful. We teach them that holiness is not about how things look, but how deeply we are willing to love. We remind ourselves, again and again, that ministry isn't for display. It's for formation. Which means it will always resist the frame.

STORIES WITHOUT STATS

There is no spreadsheet for the student who no longer cheats on tests because he finally sees integrity as part of discipleship. No data point for the junior who comes to confession not because it's required, but because he wants to start again. No year-over-year graph for the senior who still isn't sure about God, but keeps showing up to retreat meetings because he trusts you. These are the real fruits of ministry. But they don't fit into the reporting template.

When institutions ask how things are going, they usually mean: What are your numbers? How many students attended? How many were confirmed? How many photos did you post? They don't often ask: Who's healing? Who's growing? Who are you accompanying quietly through transformation? And that's the tension.

This does not call ministers to never take photos of ministry events, or to avoid asking students to reflect on their experiences, or even to measure ministry growth by participation. It is rather a call to not allow these metrics to define the measurement of a successful ministry. Because ministers see what the numbers miss. This unique vision comes from the tension lived by lay ecclesial ministers. *Christifideles Laici* challenges the laity to recognize the tension between their so-called spiritual life, and the secular life, in the lay minister, the spreadsheet and sacrament come together to form something entirely unique.[3] They see the student who hasn't made a public faith declaration but is slowly becoming more patient with his family. They notice the one who stays after Mass just a little longer than he used to. They celebrate the sophomore who stops making fun of prayer, not because he was corrected, but because something in him has softened.

---

3. *Christifideles Laici* §59

These changes are real. They are significant. But they are hard to quantify. They don't produce shareable content. They don't look impressive in a meeting. So they're often left unsaid. But the most important part of ministry rarely what happens in front of a camera. It's what happens when someone begins to live differently because they've encountered love. It's not always conversion in the dramatic sense. Sometimes it's continuity. Sometimes it's staying. Sometimes it's the slow thaw of a heart that's been frozen by cynicism, disappointment, or fear.

As ministers, we need to learn how to tell these stories. Even when they don't land with the same impact. Even when they're messy. Even when they end with "and I don't know where he is now, but I hope something took root." Because these stories matter.

They remind us why we said yes to ministry in the first place. They give us hope when everything else feels thin. And they honor the dignity of the people we serve—not as stats to be collected, but as souls in process. We may never get to write these stories into the official reports. But we can carry them in our hearts, share them in circles of trust, and let them be the quiet witness to a different kind of success. Because transformation doesn't always look like a retreat photo. Sometimes it looks like a young person, silently choosing the good. And sometimes, that's more than enough.

RETHINKING SUCCESS

If the work of ministry were evaluated by the standards Jesus used, most of our reporting templates would collapse. He never tracked attendance. He never hosted a retreat with clear outcomes. He didn't leave behind a polished succession plan or a communication strategy. Instead, He walked with twelve people and told stories that confused more than clarified. By the world's metrics, it wasn't a growth strategy. But it changed everything. That should give us pause.

In the modern Church, especially in institutions with limited time and tight budgets, the temptation is to justify ministry in terms of efficiency, reach, and visible outcomes. We build dashboards to track engagement. We emphasize the optics of joy. We seek metrics that demonstrate return on investment—whether that's enrollment, attendance, or sacramental participation. It's not that these things don't matter. It's that they were never meant to be the heart of the mission.

When we let those metrics define success, we start reshaping ministry to fit the mold. A program that fosters deep growth but low attendance is cut. A retreat that stirred hearts but lacked great photos, though considered successful in one aspect, missed the mark in another. A student who needs accompaniment over achievement gets overlooked. Slowly, the real purpose of ministry—forming disciples—gets buried beneath the pressure to prove it's working.

But what if we recalibrated? What if faithfulness became the primary measure? What if we took our late holy father seriously and leaned into the missionary option?[4] What if we asked: Did we show up? Did we listen well? Did we remain rooted in prayer? Did we plant seeds, even if we may never see them grow? Did we model what it means to follow Christ—not with fanfare, but with integrity?

That kind of success doesn't always photograph well. It doesn't always yield applause. But it is the kind that changes people, over time. It is the kind that Christ Himself embodied: patient, hidden, rooted in relationship, willing to walk with people at their own pace.[5]

It's not that we abandon accountability. We still reflect. We still evaluate. We still ask whether our efforts are bearing fruit. But we stop expecting those fruits to always be immediate, visible, or quantifiable. We learn to see formation not as an event, but as a process. Not as something we can engineer, but something we are privileged to witness and serve.

---

4. *Evangelii Gaudium* §27

5. USCCB, *Listen, Teach, Send*, 15. Quoting Pope Francis' *Christus Vivit*, the USCCB goes into great depth about the significance of Jesus' pedagogy with the disciples on the road to Emmaus in their introduction to the new framework.

Part I: What We've Inherited

That ministry is slow. That growth is unpredictable. That impact is often hidden. That the metrics we really care about—compassion, courage, fidelity, conversion—cannot be counted, but can be cultivated.

When we begin to define success that way, everything changes. The pressure eases. The work deepens. The fruits become more lasting, even if they're less flashy. And most importantly, we become more faithful to the One who called us—not to produce, but to love.

Chapter 3

Culture of Substitution

THE STAND-IN MENTALITY

There's an unspoken job description that follows many lay ministers around: "Do what needs to be done—because no one else will." Whether or not it's ever put into writing, the expectation becomes clear fast. You are the retreat coordinator, the bulletin writer, the team builder, the setup crew, the cleanup crew, the one who fills in when the deacon is out, when the youth minister quits, when the choir director gets tired, when the priest forgets to show up for adoration. Whatever the role, you are expected to hold the space.

At first, this might feel like trust. You're being asked to take ownership, to make decisions, to carry weight. But very quickly, the cracks start to show. You're responsible for carrying out the mission, but you're rarely asked how that mission should evolve. You're allowed to run the program, but not to shape the values that program serves. And you're commended for stepping up only in the moments when someone else has stepped away.

This culture of substitution is easy to miss because it often hides under the appearance of delegation. But true delegation shares decisions. Substitution just shifts the burden. When clergy are overextended, or families disengaged, or peers disinterested,

Part I: What We've Inherited

the lay minister becomes the person everyone leans on—not because it's strategic, but because it's convenient.

At school Masses, it's common for things to go sideways. The slides aren't timed right. The presider changes the readings at the last minute. The microphones cut out without warning. Student lectors bail or panic. Sometimes I find myself cueing music, calming down a nervous reader, coordinating with the priest, and checking in with tech—all within five minutes of Mass starting. We just roll with it, because we have to. And when it goes well, no one sees the chaos. They just see that it happened. That the machine kept moving.

Or take the Emmaus retreat—an overnight experience that's been running in more or less the same way for years. No one's stopping me from changing it. In theory, I could redesign it entirely. But the thought of overhauling something so ingrained feels overwhelming. I find myself thinking, Just get through it. Three more weeks. Just get to the bus. The dream of what it could be is drowned out by the pressure of keeping it afloat one more time. And so I repeat a version of the same retreat, not because it's the best version, but because there isn't time, space, or bandwidth to imagine something new.

Those moments aren't isolated. They mirror a broader pattern in ministry where structure is inherited, urgency is constant, and discernment gets sidelined. Substitution becomes not just a strategy, but a mindset. It forms the atmosphere in which lay ministers operate, quietly reminding us that we are always one absence away from another responsibility.

Worse still, this substitution isn't always recognized. Because you made the event happen. Because the sacraments were celebrated. Because the calendar didn't break. But the cost to the minister is cumulative. You become the one who always steps in—but never steps up into real influence. You become the duct tape in a system that keeps adding weight without addressing its structural faults.

Over time, this creates a dangerous kind of credibility. You're known as dependable. You're known as flexible. You're known as someone who will "figure it out." And so you're never asked what would make ministry whole again. You're only asked to make it work for one more year.

Lay ministry was never meant to be patchwork. It was never meant to be reactive. When we treat lay ministers as spiritual substitutes rather than collaborative leaders, we diminish not just their potential, but the Church's capacity to respond meaningfully to this moment. We turn vocation into vacancy-filling. We reduce leadership to logistical coverage. And we keep wondering why nothing feels alive.

Ministry will always involve stepping into the gap. But it cannot stop there. If we do not begin inviting lay ministers into the work of redesigning the system itself, we will only ever be as strong as our last substitution.

DISENGAGED PARENTS, ABSENT CLERGY

There's a fine line between being helpful and being relied upon in a way that drains your vocation. I suspect most lay ministers cross that line within their first year.

It often begins with a single yes. "Could you help set up the chairs before the parent meeting?" Of course. "Could you lead the closing prayer?" Absolutely. "Can you coordinate that event this year since you're already involved?" Sure, happy to.

At first, each request seems manageable. Reasonable, even. But something shifts over time. What began as occasional help becomes assumed availability. The invitations become expectations. And the more you say yes, the less visible your effort becomes. You stop being noticed for your willingness and start being expected for your presence. Your name is no longer one of several. It becomes the default. Suddenly, your helpfulness is no longer a gift. It's a habit—one that the system depends on, but does not support.

At a parish once, we hosted an event called the Living Stations of the Cross. It had always been a volunteer-led ministry—something laypeople from the community coordinated out of devotion and passion. But when the lead volunteer stepped down, the responsibility didn't disappear. It quietly shifted. Without discussion

Part I: What We've Inherited

or formal reassignment, it landed on my desk. Not because I had asked for it. Not because it clearly aligned with my role. But simply because there was no one else. It was a beautiful tradition. And it was now mine.

This is how lay ministers become absorbed into the institution's muscle memory. We're not just available—we're woven into the assumed fabric of how things get done. And because the outcomes often look seamless from the outside, no one questions how much hidden effort is required to keep things running. But seamlessness can be a spiritual danger. It masks the human cost. It hides the late nights, the skipped meals, the emotional weight of constantly feeling one dropped detail away from public failure. It conceals the fact that most ministry structures were not built to share work—they were built to assign it to whoever is left standing.

Eventually, your yes doesn't feel like a gift anymore. It feels like a script you don't remember agreeing to. The habit of help can turn into a cycle of quiet erosion. Your creativity shrinks. Your initiative dulls. Your sense of calling blurs. Not because you no longer care, but because you've been conscripted into a version of ministry that rewards compliance more than collaboration.

We need to name this pattern. Because unacknowledged overextension isn't holiness. It's unsustainable. And it's one of the hidden reasons so many lay ministers leave—not with a dramatic exit, but with a slow fading out of joy.

THE DOUBLE BURDEN OF EXECUTION AND BLAME

When a liturgy falls flat, a retreat underwhelms, or a service project gets canceled, there's a quiet tendency to look in one direction: the minister who executed it. Rarely does anyone ask who else was—or wasn't—in the room when the decisions were made.

Lay ministers are often tasked with delivering events, programs, or initiatives they had little role in shaping. They inherit goals, timelines, and expectations, often without the authority to revise or redirect them. Yet when the outcomes don't match the hopes, the disappointment tends to land squarely on their shoulders. Not always or even often with confrontation, but with silence, avoidance, or soft exclusion.

It's a subtle but deeply felt dynamic. You're invited to lead, but only within the bounds of someone else's framework. You're trusted with responsibility, but not with authorship. And when something doesn't succeed, the institution rarely investigates its own role in the failure. It investigates yours.

At school, we hold reconciliation services during class time, rotating students through to receive the sacrament. The only way to make it work with our schedule is to disrupt the normal rotation, and while we plan carefully, it's never a smooth operation. Sometimes a priest cancels at the last minute, and we're left scrambling—extending confession times, re-routing students, and sending them back late. Teachers and administrators grow frustrated with the disruption. But rarely does anyone ask why it happened, or who didn't show. The assumption is simple: ministry ran late, and that must mean someone dropped the ball. Even when the reason is obvious, the frustration lands on the person who had to make it work.

Or take our Kairos retreat. One tradition involves playing songs before and after each student and adult talk. These aren't just filler—they're meant to serve as bookends, anchoring the emotional and spiritual tone of the reflections. We let students choose their own songs, giving them a chance to make the talk even more their own. Some teachers, especially alumni who've led Kairos before as students, don't love this. They want songs with direct lyrical ties to the content. They've voiced this concern—just not to me. The critiques surface in conversations I'm not in, or evaluations I never see. The implication is clear: someone didn't think this through, someone let go of tradition. But no one asks what the students needed. No one asks what the moment called for.

This dynamic creates an exhausting double burden: you must deliver success, and you must absorb blame. You must carry the mission, but only on terms you didn't set. You're trusted to drive the bus but not to decide the route—or even whether the tires are good.

Part I: What We've Inherited

Over time, ministers internalize this imbalance. We grow hesitant to take risks. We shrink from creative ideas. We begin to aim for safe outcomes, ones that can't backfire or get flagged. The mission narrows. The vision dims. The work becomes about not messing up, instead of bearing fruit. And still, we are told: do more, fix more, fill more gaps. What we're also told: you're not supposed to carry this alone. Told this, but that reality is rarely lived out.

WHEN SUBSTITUTION BECOMES A CULTURE

Stopgap solutions have a way of becoming standard practice. What begins as a temporary fill-in—"Just run this event until we find someone else"—becomes the job. A small favor turns into an ongoing responsibility. A one-time absence becomes a long-term vacancy. Slowly, substitution isn't the exception anymore. It's the rule. This is the quiet evolution of dysfunction in ministry: when filling in becomes built in.

What makes this dangerous isn't just the accumulation of responsibilities—it's the erosion of clarity. No one quite knows who is responsible for what anymore. The retreat is your job now, because you've always done it. The communication plan? Yours too. The coordination of the service project, the Advent mission, the altar server training? You've touched them before, so they must be under your care. In the absence of formal support, assumption fills the gap. It's difficult to say no, because no one ever formally asked you to say yes. There's nothing to push back on, because there was never a clear boundary. There was only the growing silence of others who once held the task—or who never did to begin with.

A colleague of mine was once placed in charge of the school's Christian service program. He was given the official title and a modest stipend—but his teaching load, six full sections of senior theology, remained unchanged. The person who held the role before him had only taught two or three classes, but those adjustments weren't carried forward. He wasn't asked whether the model needed updating, or whether the structure still made sense. He was simply expected to continue what had been handed to him.

And though he had a deep passion for service, he quickly found himself boxed in—tasked with overseeing a program he had no time to reshape. He brought his concerns to leadership and felt heard, emotionally—but little changed practically. What began as a new role quickly turned into a stagnant one: responsible but voiceless, titled but unsupported.

Substitution becomes culture when everyone forgets there was ever another way. And as it becomes normalized, creativity dries up. There's no room to dream when you're stuck in the cycle of sustaining. You stop asking what could be. You start asking only what's needed to survive the week. The job becomes one long string of obligations, each bleeding into the next. Ministry is reduced to maintenance. This culture doesn't just exhaust people. It obscures the mission.

When ministers are running on fumes, the deeper goals of formation—trust, accompaniment, real growth—begin to slip. We plan programs we no longer believe in. We teach truths we don't have time to wrestle with ourselves. We ask for reflection from students we've barely had time to greet. And through it all, we pretend that this is what ministry is supposed to be. It's not. The heart of ministry is not substitution. It's communion.

We are not meant to be a backfill for broken systems. We are meant to be co-builders of the Kingdom. And until that becomes the expectation—not just the hope—we will continue to burn through ministers while wondering why nothing ever really changes.

RECOVERING A SENSE OF CALL

The more ministry becomes defined by substitution, the more ministers begin to lose their sense of call. There is a very unique vocation of lay people, one which clergy cannot lean into, by nature of their ordination. This call, to ministry in parking lots, in cafeterias, at baseball games, makes "the Church present and operative in those places and circumstances where only through them can it become the salt of the earth."[1] When every effort feels reactive, every task inherited, and every responsibility assumed rather than discerned, it becomes harder to remember why you said yes in the first place.

Vocation cannot survive in a culture of passive acceptance. It needs clarity. It needs boundaries. It needs to be rooted in mission—not just in what needs to get done, but in why we're doing it. This isn't a call for less generosity. It's a call for more intention. A lay minister who says yes to everything risks losing the ability to say yes to the right things. When all energy is spent holding up a crumbling structure, there is little left for real accompaniment, spiritual listening, or growth.

To recover a sense of call is to name what's broken—not to be cynical, but to be faithful. The Psalmist in Psalm 42 recalls a similar event, "My tears have been my food day and night, while people say to me continually, 'Where is your God?' These things I remember, as I pour out my soul: how I went with the throng, and led them in procession to the house of God,"[2] He laments while at the same time remembering the times in which he led the congregation towards God, and yet now they ask where is his God.

This challenge of reclaiming our vocation is to reclaim ministry as a chosen response to the Spirit's invitation, not just a patch for everyone else's absence. If we want ministers who lead with conviction, creativity, and joy, we have to make room for them to lead from vocation—not from obligation.

---

1. *Lumen Gentium* §33
2. Psalm 42: 2–3

Chapter 4

Good Enough to Run It, Not Enough to Change It

WHEN IMPLEMENTATION REPLACES IMAGINATION

MINISTRY PLANNING MEETINGS OFTEN begin with a blank calendar and end with it filled. A retreat date here. A reconciliation service there. A schoolwide Mass on this feast day, a parent night on that one. The year takes shape quickly, decisions made and tasks delegated. No one says it out loud, but the expectation is clear: once the vision has been declared, it's your job to make it real. It doesn't matter if the timing is poor or if the student leaders aren't ready. It doesn't matter if the same group of volunteers has already said no three times. It doesn't matter if the event no longer makes spiritual sense in your current context. It's on the calendar, so now it's on your plate.

This is the trap: the belief that success in ministry comes from flawless implementation, not faithful discernment. It's a mode of leadership where initiative is welcome only if it fits into a predetermined structure. You can suggest edits, but only if they don't cause delay. You can raise concerns, but only if you have a backup plan. Your creativity is welcome—but only within the lines.

The result is a minister who is praised for efficiency but rarely trusted with vision. You become a master of logistics, coordinating

Part I: What We've Inherited

bus schedules and ordering sacramental supplies, while feeling increasingly disconnected from the heart of the work. You know how to run the program. But you're rarely asked how, or whether it should be run at all.

Over time, this pattern forms a script. "Can you make this happen?" becomes the default invitation. "What do you think we should do?" slowly disappears. Instead of discernment, there is delegation. Instead of collaboration, there is execution. And what might have been a deeply formative ministry begins to feel like a service role—helpful, reliable, efficient, and entirely peripheral to the real decisions.

In this trap, the minister becomes a kind of spiritual event planner. The mission becomes a schedule. The vision becomes a checklist. And the heart of the work—accompaniment, trust-building, spiritual listening—is squeezed into whatever space remains after the tasks are done.

The irony is that most ministers entered this work precisely because they care about the heart. They wanted to build something meaningful. They wanted to help form disciples, walk with the hurting, create spaces for grace. But somewhere along the way, the invitation to help turned into an obligation to execute. And the deeper questions—about what's working, what's not, and what the Spirit might be asking—got buried under email threads and clipboard signups.

When a minister's role is reduced to implementation without input, burnout is not a possibility—it's a guarantee. Because what sustains ministry isn't *just* mission; it's ownership.[1] And without it, even the most well-run program will begin to feel hollow.

We are called to be leaders in the Church. That leadership will always exist under the authority of the pastor, the shepherd of the parish, whose role is to guide the vision and safeguard the mission. His discernment carries weight. But he also hired us for a reason. Our presence is not ornamental—it's intentional. We were brought on to contribute, to collaborate, to listen to the Spirit at work in the community. Leadership in the Church means not just carrying out

---

1. USCCB, *Listen, Teach, Send*, 48.

someone else's plan, but discerning together what is truly needed. It means asking whether the event we've always done still serves the people we're trying to reach. It means having the freedom to say no, or not yet, or not like this—always in communion, always in charity, but not in silence. Otherwise, we're not ministering. We're managing.

WHEN COLLABORATION ISN'T COMMUNION

One of the most common phrases in institutional ministry life is: "We'd love your input." On the surface, it sounds promising—like an invitation to real dialogue, a chance to help shape direction. But too often, that input is requested only after decisions have already been made. The meeting is framed as collaborative, yet the framework, timeline, and goals are already set. Your role is to affirm, tweak, and implement—not to discern. It's not that collaboration is absent. It's that it arrives too late to matter.

A new program is launched, and ministers are brought in to run it. A retreat theme is chosen, and then the team is asked to build talks around it. A liturgy schedule is created, and then the minister is asked to fill the roles. In each case, the appearance of collaboration is maintained—but the opportunity to shape the deeper vision has long passed. The structure is fixed. The calendar is locked. You are included, but not empowered.

This kind of pseudo-collaboration is subtle, but corrosive. It creates the illusion of shared leadership while reinforcing a top-down dynamic. Lay ministers may be asked to share their thoughts, but only within the limits of an already defined outcome. They may be included in planning meetings, but only to smooth implementation. The real decisions happen elsewhere.

Over time, this pattern trains ministers to stop offering big ideas. You learn that visioning is not your lane. You stop naming problems you can't fix. You focus on logistics and leave the rest alone. Your energy shifts from asking "What is God calling us to?" to asking "How can I make this work?" Ministry narrows from discernment to execution. From shared mission to personal output.

Part I: What We've Inherited

In some ways, this dynamic is a defense mechanism. Institutions move slowly. Real collaboration takes time and trust. It means embracing tension, risking disagreement, and opening space for co-discernment. For some leaders, that's simply too much. It feels easier to define the goal and delegate the process—to invite buy-in without relinquishing control. But that's not collaboration. That's outsourcing.

At first glance, strong oversight can seem like a responsible approach to ministry. After all, shouldn't there be accountability for what is taught, planned, and carried out in the name of the Church? Isn't it prudent to ensure consistency, theological soundness, and alignment with pastoral goals? Of course. Oversight is essential. But when oversight crosses into micromanagement—when vision is dictated rather than discerned together—the unintended consequences begin to stack up.

Innovation dies quickly in environments of constant approval-seeking. Lay ministers, especially newer ones, often arrive with creative energy: fresh retreat formats, new service initiatives, outreach models that respond to students' actual lives. But when every idea must run a gauntlet of gatekeeping, that energy fades. Not because the ideas weren't good—but because the process for bringing them to life was too steep, too slow, or too closed.

Eventually, people stop offering ideas altogether. They do what worked last year, or what was asked for directly. Not because they believe it's the most fruitful approach, but because it's safe. Predictable. Endorsed. Control rewards compliance, not creativity. What's more, this culture of control communicates something deeper and more disheartening: that ministers are not fully trusted.

It's hard to give your heart to a ministry that doesn't trust your judgment. Even harder when you're the one on the front lines—listening to students' doubts, noticing who's drifting, and seeing the slow erosion of engagement. Lay ministers often have the clearest read on what is spiritually needed, precisely because they're immersed in the pastoral fabric of the community. But when those insights are consistently overridden or dismissed, it creates a gap between what's real and what's expected.

And over time, that gap breeds quiet dissonance. Ministers begin to wonder: Do they really want formation here—or just a polished program? Do they really want evangelization—or just attendance? Do they want mission—or maintenance?

The more the system values control, the less it can hear the people closest to the work. Ministries become rigid. Programs repeat themselves. Honest feedback is avoided. New ideas are treated as threats. And when something falters, the blame is rarely directed upward—it falls on the person tasked with making it work.

Meanwhile, the spiritual needs of the people go unmet. The event runs smoothly, but no one is transformed. The program is implemented, but no one feels known. The retreat is approved, but the structure hasn't changed in years. The irony is that institutions often exercise control in the name of protecting the mission. But too much control actually prevents the ministry from responding to that mission. The real work of accompaniment is dynamic, contextual, and rooted in trust.[2] It requires room to adapt, to risk, to respond.

When ministers are trusted—truly trusted—they tend to rise to the challenge. They take ownership. They bring creativity. They become more—not less—accountable. But when their work is subject to constant interference or second-guessing, they learn to retreat. Not from the mission, but from the parts of it they can't shape.

Without real collaboration, ministry becomes something done for ministers, not with them. And without trust, collaboration becomes just another checkbox—another illusion in a Church that was meant to be a communion.

FALSE AUTONOMY, REAL EXHAUSTION

"I trust your judgment—just keep me updated." It sounds like support. On paper, it reads as empowerment. But in practice, it often means being left alone to carry a vision that wasn't yours, toward outcomes you didn't define, with very little help along the way. This is the paradox of lay ministry in many parishes and schools

---

2. USCCB, *Listen, Teach, Send*, 19–23.

Part I: What We've Inherited

today: freedom in theory, constraint in practice. Ministers are told they have autonomy. They're encouraged to be creative, to "own" their programs. Yet when a retreat doesn't meet attendance expectations, or a service project fails to hit a target number of volunteers, the accountability comes crashing down—not to clarify, but to critique.

You're free—until the numbers drop. You're trusted—until someone complains. You're autonomous—until the optics falter. This dynamic is one of the most disorienting and exhausting aspects of ministry leadership. It creates a felt sense of risk without support. You are responsible for producing results, but not empowered to shape the environment that makes those results possible. You're held to metrics you didn't choose, operating within structures you didn't build, asked to explain outcomes you couldn't fully influence.

Over time, this breeds a quiet dissonance. You tell yourself you're doing ministry. But your days are filled with managing spreadsheets, troubleshooting logistics, and preemptively addressing complaints. The deeper questions—Are students actually growing in faith? Are we creating space for encounter?—get pushed to the margins, because the institutional demands are louder.

The dissonance grows when you realize that your work is being evaluated on optics more than impact. You could spend hours in one-on-one conversation with a struggling teen, walk with them through grief, help them rediscover prayer—and that encounter will be invisible to most. But if you forget to post a picture from the retreat, or if signups are low, someone notices.

So you work harder. You overfunction. You try to keep the peace, hit the marks, and still carve out space for what matters. But the energy it takes to maintain this dual consciousness—to be both faithful and performative, authentic and strategic—starts to erode your interior life.

Eventually, you start making choices not based on what's most formative, but on what will draw the least scrutiny. You avoid risks. You stick with what's been approved before. You limit your vision to what won't require fighting for. And slowly, almost imperceptibly, your sense of spiritual leadership gives way to a low-grade institutional survival mode. This is not freedom. It's burnout in slow motion.

The great irony is that this model doesn't even serve the parish well. Ministries built on false autonomy and unrealistic expectations do not flourish. They survive—until the minister can no longer carry it. If institutions want real results—spiritual, transformative, lasting—they have to offer real trust. Not just the illusion of freedom, but the conditions that make it meaningful: clear support, shared ownership, honest dialogue, and a willingness to revise the structure when it no longer serves the mission. Without that, what looks like autonomy is just abandonment with a flattering name. And the exhaustion it produces is not a sign of weakness—it's a sign that the system isn't honest about what it demands.

RECLAIMING CO-RESPONSIBILITY

If we want lay ministry to be sustainable—and more than that, to be spiritually fruitful—we have to reclaim ownership. Not in the sense of individual control, but in the deeper sense of shared mission. Ministry cannot thrive when lay leaders are treated as contractors brought in to execute someone else's blueprint. Nor can they flourish a vague mission statement and no ongoing support. It flourishes when vision is discerned together, when direction is shaped in communion, and when leadership is distributed across the body of Christ.

This is not about flattening all hierarchy or pretending that everyone's voice carries the same weight in every decision. The pastor, as the shepherd of the parish, retains the final responsibility for guiding the community's mission and maintaining its unity. His leadership is vital. But he does not lead alone. A healthy parish culture draws upon the diverse gifts of its ministers and trusts them not only to carry out the work, but to help shape it.

Co-responsibility means cultivating a culture where discernment matters as much as delivery—where ministers are trusted to name needs, surface insights, and co-author the very work they are expected to lead. Ownership means being involved in the "why," not just the "how." It means institutions that listen before assigning, that reflect before mandating, and that value spiritual formation as much as they value operational success.

This shift doesn't happen all at once. It begins with one honest conversation, one act of trust, one space where the minister is invited to speak not just as a doer, but as a co-discerner of God's will for the community. That's the kind of culture where lay ministry can stop surviving—and start bearing lasting fruit.

Accompaniment Meditation I

This book has been naming some of the invisible tensions of lay ministry from a structural level. But sometimes, the most painful moments aren't systemic. They're personal, quiet, and hard to describe to someone who doesn't live in this work. Here's some of those moments.

THE EMAIL YOU NEVER GOT A REPLY TO

You had an idea. A good one. You drafted it carefully. A new ministry night, maybe. A retreat follow-up gathering. A simple way to build momentum off something that had gone well—a conversation, a moment of grace, a student's spark of interest. You thought, This could matter.

So you emailed. You made it easy to say yes. Clear. Respectful. Aligned with the mission. You even offered to coordinate the details, knowing everyone's busy. You hit send with hope, not entitlement. You weren't asking for praise—just partnership.

And then? Nothing. No reply. No follow-up. No "We're swamped, but thanks." Just silence.

You check your inbox later that day. Then the next. Then a week later. You wonder if they saw it. You reread what you wrote—was it too long? Too soon? Too much? You tell yourself, "It's not personal." But it is personal. Because it was your effort. Your attempt to build something real. And now it's sitting unopened in someone else's inbox, already stale.

The students ask about it. "Are we still doing that thing?" You stall. You say you're waiting to hear back. You try not to let the uncertainty show. Eventually, you let the idea die. Not because it wasn't good. Not because it wouldn't have borne fruit. But because you couldn't do it alone—and no one else even said, "Let's try."

That silence at the start? It becomes something heavier than rejection. It becomes a pattern. It becomes a quiet inner voice that says, don't bother next time. You learn to pitch smaller. To ask for less. To hold back the full vision, because casting it wide has only ever left you standing alone.

That's how ministry shrinks. Not through failure. But through absence. Through invitations unanswered, support unstated, potential unacknowledged.

Through the email you never got a reply to.

THE PHOTO THAT WASN'T TAKEN

There was a moment. A real one. It wasn't on the calendar. It didn't happen at a microphone or under a spotlight. It wasn't planned or staged. It didn't even last long. But for a few minutes, something holy passed between you and a student.

Maybe it was after a talk when everyone else was laughing and heading to small groups, and one kid hung back. Maybe it was in the chapel during Adoration, when someone who never closes his eyes suddenly did. Maybe it was in a classroom after the bell, when a student who never speaks said, "Can I ask you something?"

No one took a photo. No one wrote it down. It wasn't loud enough to make the highlight reel. But it stayed with you. You remember the way the student looked—not dramatic, not weeping, just present in a way you hadn't seen before. You remember the question they asked, or the look in their eyes when you told them, "You're not alone."

You didn't post about it. You didn't have time to turn it into a caption, or think to take a picture. And even if you had, it wouldn't have captured what actually happened.

Accompaniment Meditation I

How do you photograph trust? How do you capture quiet courage?

You don't. You live it. You carry it.

But later, someone asks how the event went. And you hesitate. You know what they're really asking: Did it look good? Did people show up? Did we get content for the newsletter? You say it went well. You mention the turnout. You nod toward the bulletin board of photos from the lunch beforehand. You don't mention the moment that really mattered. It wouldn't translate.

There are no numbers for grace. No spreadsheet cell that can hold that kind of depth. Still, you think about it for days. You pray for that student. You wonder if it will be the start of something. Maybe it won't. But for one moment, they felt seen. They felt loved. And you were lucky enough to witness it. You don't need a photo to remember. Because that moment—that flash of presence, honesty, and holiness—was ministry at its most real.

THE METRICS YOU DON'T REPORT

There's no form for this. No place on the report to write: He came back to confession after three years. No dropdown menu for: She finally forgave her dad. No checkbox that says: She stayed after to pray when everyone else went to lunch.

These are the fruits that never make the spreadsheet. But they're the ones you carry with you. A senior who never takes faith seriously lingers after a retreat, just long enough to say, "I think I want to come to Mass again." A student who usually sits in the back cracks a joke during small group. Everyone laughs. You realize it's the first time he's spoken in two days. A girl who hasn't smiled all semester sends a one-sentence email: Thank you for today.

You can't quantify it. You can't log it in the year-end summary. You try, sometimes. You write "positive student feedback" in your notes. You drop hints in the department meeting. You mention the student who asked a thoughtful question, hoping it'll count for something.

But deep down, you know it won't. The metrics are built for programs, not people. They track engagement, not transformation. They look for graphs that go up and to the right. But growth in grace isn't linear. And it rarely performs on schedule.

So you develop a second memory. A shadow spreadsheet, just for yourself. You remember the student who cried during worship. You remember the breakthrough conversation. You remember the small reconciliations no one else saw.

They're not impressive. But they're real. They're not public. But they're personal. They're not scalable. But they're sacred. And they're why you stay. Not for the metrics you can report. But for the ones that remind you: something is still happening here, even if no one else sees it.

STILL HERE

You walk into another empty classroom, holding a clipboard no one asked for. You've already done this presentation twice today. The first one barely looked up from their desks. The second went okay, you think. It's hard to tell.

You straighten the chairs. Rearrange the handouts. Adjust the projector that never quite works. You tell yourself it matters. Because maybe this time it will. No one asked you to give this talk. But you know no one else will. No one's expecting a miracle. But you've learned that grace doesn't need a crowd.

The weight is still there. The exhaustion of doing the unseen, unasked, uncelebrated work. The pressure to make it happen even when no one helps make it possible. The inbox is still full of unanswered requests. The staff meetings still skate past the faith formation report. The parents still don't reply.

But you show up anyway. Not because you're naive. Not because you think today will be the day it all turns around. But because you've seen what happens when you keep showing up. You've seen the quiet kid finally volunteer. You've seen the one who rolled their eyes last week stop and ask a real question. You've

Accompaniment Meditation I

seen the ones who swore they'd never come back stand with their hands open in prayer.

And even when you don't see it—when there's no moment, no fruit, no sign—you keep showing up. Because presence is its own witness. Because showing up says, You still matter to me. This still matters to me. Because Christ keeps showing up in the Eucharist, whether or not we're paying attention.

You've learned to match that kind of faithfulness. So you set the chairs again. You reset the slideshow. You take a deep breath, smile at the first student who walks in, and begin.

Because you're still here. So much of ministry happens in these quiet moments. They don't make the annual report. But they are the reason we stay.

Part II

What They're Really Leaving

Chapter 5

Beyond Performance-Based Belonging

PART 1 OF THIS book named the quiet burden that many lay ministers carry: the exhaustion of responsibility without authority, the spiritual cost of substitution culture, the frustration of performative metrics, and the disillusionment of being trusted to execute but not to discern. These aren't isolated grievances—they're signs of a system that has stopped listening to the people closest to the work. But the consequences of this dysfunction aren't limited to those in leadership roles. They ripple outward. When ministers are forced to run programs they didn't shape, when formation is replaced with logistics, when burnout is rewarded as commitment—the ministry itself becomes thin. And those we're trying to reach, especially young people, begin to sense that thinness. Part 2 explores what that looks like on the ground: not just why young people are leaving, but how our current ministry structures often fail to invite them into real belonging. Because the spiritual fatigue of ministers and the disaffiliation of the next generation are not separate stories. They are two sides of the same ecclesial wound.

PARTICIPATION ISN'T BELONGING

There's a familiar rhythm to the way young people are often invited into the life of the Church. A youth Mass needs lectors, so a few students are asked to read. A retreat needs a witness talk, so someone charismatic is chosen. A service event needs volunteers, so a sign-up sheet is passed around during theology class. These are real forms of involvement. But involvement alone does not equate to belonging.

Too often, participation is mistaken for communion. We see students at the event, behind the ambo, on the retreat team—and we assume they feel part of the Church. Sometimes they do. But just as often, they show up because someone asked them to, or because it looks good on college applications, or because they've been formed to associate faith with tasks. When the task ends, so does their presence.[1]

Participation without formation is a shallow well. It offers a temporary sense of purpose but rarely provides the spiritual depth that sustains conviction. Likewise, participation without trust signals that a young person's role is to serve a predetermined vision—not to help discern or shape it.

In my own experience, there's a persistent pattern I've come to call the "plug-in" model. There's a spot to fill—a retreat team member, a lector, a small group leader—and we slot someone in. They're given a responsibility, a checklist, and maybe a t-shirt. But what they're not often given is the space to ask real questions, to reflect on why the role matters, or to connect it to their sense of calling. Instead of treating them as companions on a journey of formation, we treat them as functional parts of a system that needs to keep running. Because it does. It would take an immense amount of force to stop this machine, and just as much to get it running again.

Even the language we use can reinforce this. We speak of "getting kids involved," "making sure they show up," "giving them something to do." Rarely do we ask whether they've been given the space to grow. When faith is tied primarily to participation, rather than transformation, we shouldn't be surprised when they walk away once the event is over. They weren't walking away from the

---

1. Springtide Research Institute, *Belonging*, 37–44

faith. They were stepping out of a system that never invited them into ownership in the first place.

This can be especially disorienting for young people who have genuine questions, spiritual hunger, or a desire to lead. When their desire for depth is met with performance-based expectations—"read this, sing that, give this talk"—they learn to separate public involvement from personal faith. They may continue to serve out of habit or obligation, but the internal disconnect grows. And then, eventually, they leave. Not in anger. Not in rebellion. In silence.

We call it disaffiliation. But often, it's the result of never having been truly affiliated to begin with. If we want to invite young people into lasting communion with the Church, we have to go beyond offering roles and start offering relationship. That means trusting them with questions. Walking with them in ambiguity. Letting them see the messy, human side of ministry. It means formation that takes time and vulnerability. It means asking what they think the Church is called to be, and listening as if their answers matter.

Young people don't just want to be on the roster. They want to know they belong.[2] That belonging doesn't begin with participation. It begins with presence, with conversation, with mutual trust. It begins when we stop using ministry roles as proof of faith and start offering faith as a path to personal meaning, shared mission, and lifelong growth.

WHAT THEY'RE ACTUALLY REJECTING

When a young person stops coming to Mass, we often assume the problem lies in their commitment, not in the environment we offered them. We label them disengaged, disinterested, even rebellious. But more often than not, they are responding—not to Christ, not to the Gospel—but to something more human and structural. They are responding to the kind of welcome they received, or didn't.

---

2. Springtide Research Institute, *Belonging*, 37.

Part II: What They're Really Leaving

For many, the Church extended a welcome that was conditional: you're welcome here as long as you fit. As long as you behave. As long as you don't raise difficult questions, push uncomfortable conversations, or disrupt the expected flow of things. It's a welcome that praises participation but expects formation to look a certain way. It accepts volunteers but is wary of voices. What young people are rejecting, in many cases, is not faith—but managed inclusion. They are turning away from the experience of being tolerated rather than trusted, spotlighted rather than heard. They were invited to be visible, but not vulnerable.

A teen is praised for giving a testimony but never asked what they actually believe. A young person is honored for their volunteer hours but feels unseen in their struggle with faith or family life. These gestures may come from a good place, but they create an environment where involvement feels like performance, and identity is flattened into utility.

There is a script. There is a format. There is little room for improvisation, for ownership, for the kind of messiness that real faith journeys include.

When they step away, we grieve the loss, but we rarely ask what they were walking away from. If we did, we might hear things like:

- "I was never allowed to talk about my doubts."
- "They didn't want my story, just my testimony."
- "It felt like I was being used to prove something."
- "They welcomed me, but only the version of me that agreed with everything."

These are not theological rejections. They are pastoral wounds.

We do damage when we assume that disaffiliation is primarily intellectual—that it stems from disbelief, relativism, or poor catechesis. While those may play a role, the deeper fracture is usually relational. It's about not being seen, not being heard, not being trusted.

Beyond Performance-Based Belonging

If we want to respond meaningfully to disaffiliation, we have to start by honoring the truth behind their departure. Many are not walking away from Christ. They're walking away from experiences of conditional belonging. They're walking away from communities that confused visibility with value, or structure with spirit.

Until we're willing to admit that, we'll keep trying to fix the wrong problem.

THE HUNGER BENEATH THE HESITATION

We often mistake silence for apathy. When a teenager shrugs off a retreat invitation or a college student stops coming to Mass, we assume they no longer care. But beneath that hesitation, there is almost always a hunger—for something real, something grounding, something worth giving their life to. The tragedy is not that they have stopped seeking. The tragedy is that they no longer think the Church has what they're looking for.

When young people say they're "spiritual but not religious," what they often mean is that they're still asking the deepest questions—they just don't trust the institutional Church to help them answer them. They want truth, but not when it's wielded as a weapon. They want connection, but not if it means being flattened into a demographic. They want mission, but not if it's reduced to a promotional campaign. They want something beautiful, something difficult, something that costs them something and changes them in return. But they don't see many communities offering that.

This is the weight that lay ministries bare. The minster must both maintain the machine, and cater to the needs of the individual before him or her. Host this retreat, run this event, or teach this class, and at the same time allow space for this young person processing the death of his grandfather, answer deep theological questions about sexual morality, or just spend time listening to a student vent about his bad day. Recall the thesis of this book: this is not an attempt to create a patchwork, one size fits all solution, in fact there will not be a solution on offer. Rather, the goal is to simply name the problem in depth.

Part II: What They're Really Leaving

Returning to the disaffiliates, they see a Church that often looks afraid of its own depth—afraid to let the questions linger, afraid to let mystery breathe. They encounter faith spaces that lean more on slogans than silence, more on slogans than witness. And so, they turn elsewhere. Some may find a version of connection through activism or artistic expression. Others pursue wellness or justice initiatives that feel more embodied and participatory than the ministries they left behind. Still others drift in quieter ways—longing for meaning, but unsure where to look for it.

When they do try to return, even briefly, their hesitations are often misread. A student who is quiet during a small group might be labeled disinterested, when in fact he's testing whether it's safe to speak honestly. A young adult who raises questions about sexuality or Church teaching might be seen as combative, when really, she's hoping someone will trust her enough to have a real conversation. The hesitation is not a lack of desire—it's a measure of past disappointment. Many of them still hope, even if they won't say it out loud.

They hope for a Church that listens before it labels. A mentor who walks with them instead of correcting them. A community that sees their gifts before their failures. They hope to be taken seriously—not as future adults of the Church, but as present members of the Body.

The question for us is whether we still recognize their longing. Whether we still believe that God is at work beneath their skepticism. Whether we are willing to be patient enough, humble enough, to meet them where they are rather than where we wish they would be. If we can't see the hunger beneath the hesitation, we'll never offer them food that satisfies.

AGENCY AS EVANGELIZATION

One of the most persistent myths in Church life is that young people will be ready to lead "someday"—after they've matured, studied more, or learned to behave properly in a pew. Until then, we give them roles that look like leadership but are really just performance: reading at Mass, passing out donuts, showing up to youth group in the right T-shirt. These are good things. But they are not agency.

Real agency in ministry means trusting someone with spiritual responsibility before they've proven themselves. It means inviting them not just to participate but to shape. Not just to echo the Church's teaching but to wrestle with it, carry it, proclaim it, and live it out in real time. That trust is not a side project. It is evangelization.

Evangelization is not primarily about teaching content or organizing events. It is about forming people who live and lead from a place of conviction, humility, and courage. And that formation cannot happen in a vacuum. It requires context, ownership, and voice. It requires the Church to believe that the Holy Spirit is speaking not just through hierarchy and tradition, but through the lives of young people now.

That means giving them actual decisions to make—and listening when their ideas differ from ours. It means handing over responsibility for retreats, prayer services, service projects, small groups, and letting them take the lead—even if it's messy, even if it's different, even if it's not quite how we would have done it. It means mentoring them, not managing them.

There's a fear that comes with this, of course. A fear that the theology won't be precise, the reflection won't be deep enough, or the tone will be off. And yes, it might be. But the bigger risk is forming generations of Catholics who never experienced the Gospel as something entrusted to them—only something handed down and enforced from above.

Agency is not something we give when we think they've earned it. It's something we offer as a condition for real growth. Because no one internalizes a faith they've only ever been asked to imitate.

In my own ministry, the most powerful moments of conversion and ownership have come not from flawless catechesis, but from messy collaboration. Students leading a retreat talk for the first time. A group of seniors creating a Stations of the Cross experience rooted in their personal prayer. A junior stepping into extraordinary ministry of the Holy Eucharist, and realizing the weight of that moment. They didn't get everything right. But they were formed—not just informed—because they were trusted.

Evangelization is not about producing better attendance. It's about producing disciples. And disciples are formed by doing what disciples do: following Jesus, taking risks, making mistakes, and growing into their call.

We do not lose control when we give young people agency. We gain partners in the Gospel.

A BELONGING THAT FORMS

The Church is not a social club with open doors—it is a body with a mission. And yet, too often, our invitation to young people stops at the threshold. We say they belong because we let them attend, smile when they walk in, or hand them a name tag. But true belonging doesn't just welcome someone into a space. It draws them into a purpose. "You are a chosen race, a royal priesthood, a holy nation, God's own people, in order that you may proclaim the mighty acts of him who called you out of darkness into his marvelous light."[3] To belong to the Church is to be called into discipleship.[4] It is to be known, formed, and sent just as Jesus sent out the seventy-two. That kind of belonging isn't passive—it asks something. It invites a young person to see their life as a site of mission, their gifts as necessary to the Church's work, and their questions as part of a living tradition.

When we stop at welcome without moving toward formation, we foster fragile faith. We create a culture where students feel included but not invested, seen but not summoned. Eventually, they drift—because nothing was ever truly asked of them.

If we want young people to stay, we have to stop trying to keep them comfortable. We have to start calling them to become. Not

---

3. 1 Peter 2:9
4. Matthew 28:19–20

Beyond Performance-Based Belonging

just warm bodies in the pews, but active bearers of the Church's mission—disciples who belong not because they're tolerated, but because they are trusted.

Chapter 6

Listening to What Disaffiliation Is Really Saying

NOT AN INTELLECTUAL EXIT

It is easy to imagine that young people leave the Church after wrestling with its teachings—grappling with moral doctrines, theological claims, or liturgical forms. That may be the story we prefer to tell, because it gives us a debate to win or a catechesis plan to improve. But more often, the reasons are quieter and more personal. It's not doctrine they are rejecting—it's distance.

This is not to say that doctrine doesn't matter or that intellectual formation isn't vital. But disaffiliation is rarely sparked by a sudden disagreement with a Church teaching.[1] It begins, more often than not, with a growing sense that one's questions are unwelcome, one's story is unheard, or one's presence is optional.[2] It grows in the silence between encounters, the months that pass without follow-up, the hollow affirmation that isn't accompanied by any real invitation to grow.

Some young people do eventually take issue with specific teachings—but that usually comes later, when the relational fabric has already worn thin. What begins as emotional or spiritual

---

1. Saint Mary's Press, *Going, Going, Gone*, 21–24.
2. Saint Mary's Press, *Going, Going, Gone*, 13–20

disengagement can evolve into theological skepticism, especially if the Church becomes associated with exclusion or indifference. But that sequence matters. They don't leave because they disagree. They disagree much more forcefully because they've already started to leave.

This insight should shift our focus. When we treat disaffiliation as a problem of catechesis alone, we miss the deeper crisis: a failure of presence. What many young people long for is not just clarity, but company. They want to know that someone will walk with them through their questions, doubts, and developmental shifts—not hover nearby with a correction ready. They need relationships that last longer than a program cycle. They need adults who remember their names, ask about their families, and make space for real conversation.

The question is not, "How can we convince them to come back?" The question is, "Did we ever really walk with them?" If we listen carefully to what disaffiliation is actually saying, we might realize it's not a rebellion. It's a lament. A lament that the Church, which should have been the most enduring relationship in their life, felt more like an event they once attended.

Until we face that grief, we cannot begin to rebuild. And we cannot face it if we keep assuming their departure is primarily doctrinal. The path home begins not with a lecture, but with a listening ear.

WHEN SILENCE SPEAKS LOUDEST

Silence is rarely neutral. In ministry, it almost always means something. A student emails a youth minister with a vulnerable question and gets no reply. A young adult reaches out about volunteering and never hears back. A parent shares a concern and is told, "We'll look into it," only for nothing to change. These may seem like administrative oversights or simple lapses in communication, but they speak volumes.

In the absence of acknowledgment, people begin to write their own conclusions. The young person whose question went unanswered assumes they asked it wrong—or worse, that they shouldn't have asked at all. The eager volunteer interprets the lack of follow-up as a lack of welcome. The parishioner who voiced a concern quietly learns that feedback isn't valued. Over time, these unspoken conclusions calcify into disconnection.

We often imagine disaffiliation as a dramatic turning away, a deliberate rejection of faith. But more often, it's a quiet drift that starts with one unanswered message, one canceled meeting, one forgotten name. It's a slow accumulation of silence. Eventually, the young person stops reaching out—not because they no longer care, but because they believe no one else does.

Ministers, too, experience this silence. When a program doesn't meet expectations and no one checks in. When a new idea is proposed and never acknowledged. When effort is poured out and the only response is institutional quiet. This silence doesn't just demoralize—it teaches. It teaches that input isn't wanted, that trust is optional, and that showing up might not be worth the cost.

And if those of us within the system are shaped by that silence, how much more so are those who have one foot out the door? The tragedy of this kind of disaffiliation is that it's so preventable. A reply. A conversation. A single act of presence. These are not heavy lifts. They are small gestures that say, "I see you. I care. You matter." And yet, the systems we work within often fail to prioritize them. We are too busy, too under-resourced, too tangled in our own administrative burdens to give the human response that could have made the difference.

There is a spiritual cost to that neglect. It erodes not only our credibility but our witness. Because the Gospel is not silent. The God we proclaim is not distant or unresponsive. If our ministry echoes back with silence, we are not merely inefficient—we are misrepresenting the One we claim to serve.

It is not enough to get the theology right if we get the relationship wrong. The silence of a Church that does not respond is often louder than the voice of any cultural critique. And for many, it is that silence—not ideology—that finally pushes them away.

THE COST OF ABSENCE

When a young person reflects on their experience of Church and struggles to name a single adult who walked with them spiritually, that's not a fluke—it's a wound. One of the most consistent findings in ministry research is that accompaniment matters. Mentorship matters. Being known matters.[3] And yet, we have built ecclesial systems where it is entirely possible to attend weekly Mass for years, complete sacramental prep programs, and participate in parish life without ever having a genuine spiritual conversation with an adult.

That absence is not just emotional—it is formational. A teenager who never receives personal mentorship does not learn how to mentor. A confirmation candidate who never feels truly listened to may associate the sacraments with compliance rather than invitation; the graduation sacrament. A young adult who asks a vulnerable question and is handed a pamphlet instead of a conversation learns that doubt is not welcome here. In the vacuum left by absent relationships, distorted understandings of Church, faith, and God take root.

What's often missed in this conversation is how these absences shape not only what young people believe but *how* they believe. When relationships are thin or transactional, the faith becomes performative. You do the things—attend, serve, smile—but you don't know why. There's no one walking beside you to ask deeper questions, to name moments of grace, or to challenge you with love. Without that, the Church becomes a place of vague obligation or shallow community—never a home.

And when people leave that kind of Church, we shouldn't be surprised. They aren't leaving a relationship—they're leaving the absence of one. This is not to say that all priests, catechists, or youth ministers are disengaged. Many are pouring themselves out in extraordinary ways. But the structure itself often undermines their efforts, and asks so much in addition. One minister can only walk with so many, especially while juggling so many

---

3. Springtide Research Institute, *Belonging*, 45–56.

simultaneous programs and events. Without a culture of shared accompaniment—where mentoring and presence are normative across the community—the burden falls on too few, and too many slip through the cracks.

The cost of this absence compounds over time. The student who never experienced real spiritual friendship doesn't know how to build it in college. The young adult who never saw adults living their faith with joy and conviction has no image of Catholic adulthood to aspire to. The person who walked away from Church with questions unresolved and grief unshared may never know that those things were meant to be part of the conversation.

And perhaps most heartbreakingly, some begin to assume that their spiritual hunger is a problem—something to keep quiet, since no one else seems to feel it. This is not the Church Christ founded. His ministry was built on presence: walking with, staying with, listening and breaking bread.[4] The early Church grew not through marketing, but through households of radical community and discipleship.[5] We do not need to reinvent the Gospel. We need to remember how it spreads: person to person, heart to heart. If we want people to stay, we have to show up.

THE VOICE IN THEIR DEPARTURE

When a young person stops showing up to youth nights, drifts away after confirmation, or quietly walks out of Church life in college, we tend to assume apathy. We chalk it up to busyness, secular influence, or laziness. But what if their departure is actually a statement? What if leaving is the only way they know how to say, "This no longer feels like home."

For many, disaffiliation is not rebellion—it's resistance. A resistance to shallow community, to spaces where they feel unseen or unsafe. It is a response to the unspoken pressures and perceived contradictions they have absorbed: Be joyful, but don't question.

---

4. Luke 24: 13–35
5. Acts 2:42–47.

Be involved, but don't lead. Be Catholic, but only on our terms. When the invitation to participate comes with unspoken limits, walking away becomes the clearest form of honesty.

We don't have to agree with every reason someone gives for leaving in order to take it seriously. The instinct to correct, defend, or explain often short-circuits what could be moments of deep insight. Sometimes the complaint is about the Church's moral teachings—but more often, it's about the way those teachings were delivered, or how compassion was withheld. Sometimes it's about the institution—but often it's about a specific moment when trust was broken, when someone didn't listen, or when silence met their suffering.

Their departure may be the only place they believe their voice will be noticed, whether or not they actively had the thought. When we stop treating disaffiliation as a problem to fix and start treating it as a cry to be heard, we begin to understand its pastoral weight. These are not data points on a trend line. These are stories—often marked by pain, confusion, disappointment, and longing. Beneath the frustration is often a deep desire for something real. Something they hoped the Church would be. Something we may have failed to show them.

There is an invitation here—not to shame, not to correct, but to listen. To listen without immediately strategizing a response. When the synod on synodality was in its information gathering phase, when parishes hosted their listening sessions, the concerns raised were of course To listen as Christ did: fully, attentively, with the kind of compassion that draws people back not because they were wrong to leave, but because they feel seen enough to return.

The Church must develop a better pastoral imagination—one that hears absence as communication and interprets distance not as failure, but as a challenge to grow. Because sometimes the only voice we can hear is the one that's walking away. And if we're brave enough to listen, it might change everything.

Part II: What They're Really Leaving

CREATING A CULTURE OF LISTENING

If we're serious about reaching the disaffiliated, we must stop assuming that better branding or bigger events will bring them back. What's needed is something much quieter—and much more difficult. We need a culture of listening.

Listening is not passive. It is a spiritual discipline that requires presence, humility, and interior strength. It requires us to sit with discomfort, to resist defensiveness, and to hear what someone is actually saying—not what we hope they mean. Pope Francis describes listening quite poetically,

> "We need to practice the art of listening, which is more than simply hearing. Listening, in communication, is an openness of heart which makes possible that closeness without which genuine spiritual encounter cannot occur. Listening helps us to find the right gesture and word which shows that we are more than simply bystanders."[6]

When young people express frustration or distance from the Church, their honesty must be received as a gift, not a threat.

But too often, our response is a program. We create new initiatives, launch new themes, add new speaker series—as if energy alone can substitute for empathy. Yet a parish calendar full of events means little if no one feels safe enough to share their story. A Church serious about listening must prove, in concrete ways, that every voice matters—even the ones that challenge us.

This means making room for questions that don't have tidy answers. It means building teams that include people who've wrestled with doubt or felt like outsiders. It means slowing down enough to ask, "What have you experienced?" before asking, "How can we bring you back?"

In many ways, Jesus already modeled this. He listened to the woman at the well before telling her who He was.[7] He asked the blind man what he wanted, even though the answer was obvious.[8]

---

6. *Evangelii Gaudium* §171
7. John 4:1–42
8. John 9:1–12

Listening to What Disaffiliation Is Really Saying

He walked with the disciples on the road to Emmaus, letting them speak first—even though He held the answer to their sorrow.[9] Divine listening creates space for dignity to reemerge. That's the kind of Church people want to come back to. One that listens not out of strategy, but out of love. And the culture that can hold that kind of listening doesn't start with a program. It starts with us.

---

9. Luke 24:13–48

Chapter 7

Institutional Silence

THE SILENCE AFTER THE EVENT

The retreat ends. The supplies are packed. The last van is returned. The evaluations are filed—if there were any. You've dropped students off, made sure they got home safe, and maybe even lingered to pray before heading back to your office. You wait, just for a moment, for something to arrive in return. A text from a colleague, a note from your administrator, a question from someone who wondered how it all went. But it doesn't come.

There is a kind of silence in ministry that doesn't sound hostile, but feels like erasure. It comes not in the form of critique, but in the absence of response. No follow-up conversation. No hallway check-in. No "thanks for leading that." No "how did it go?" Just the slow, quiet return to normal—almost as if the event never happened.

Ministers rarely expect praise. Most of us don't need fanfare or applause. But what we do long for—sometimes desperately—is shared meaning. A sign that what we gave mattered. That someone noticed. That something stayed with them. Instead, we are often left to narrate our own experience in isolation, unsure whether the effort was invisible, insufficient, or simply irrelevant to the wider community.

Institutional Silence

Even the most spiritually rich moments—students crying in reconciliation, volunteers sharing deep prayer, spontaneous acts of leadership—can feel like they vanish into the void once the event ends. These are the moments that we hoped would ripple outward, the ones that affirmed why we said yes to this work in the first place. But without anyone to hold them with us, they start to feel like secrets we're not allowed to share. If no one acknowledges them, did they even count?

The problem is not just emotional—it's institutional. When ministry is structurally isolated, its fruits are easily siloed. The retreat team isn't asked to debrief with the academic team. Liturgy prep doesn't get folded into the staff meeting. Students return to classrooms where no one references the Mass they just participated in. Over time, the disconnect becomes routine. The retreat is "your thing." The liturgy is "your job." And because it's "yours," the rest of the institution quietly takes its hands off.

Silence doesn't only follow failure. It follows success too—if that success doesn't fit into someone else's framework of what's important. You can lead a beautiful retreat, but if it doesn't raise enrollment, solve a disciplinary issue, or align with the latest branding push, it may not register. You can accompany a student through a powerful spiritual breakthrough, but if that student still struggles in class or doesn't volunteer publicly, the moment stays invisible.

This institutional silence erodes more than morale. It muddies clarity. It leaves the minister wondering, "What matters here?" Is it transformation—or just participation? Depth—or just deliverables? We begin to second-guess not just our work, but our instincts. If no one asks about the fruit, should I stop planting? If no one shares the story, should I stop telling it?

Over time, this silence becomes a kind of spiritual static—dulling courage, flattening vision, and making it harder to believe that what we do has lasting meaning. It tempts us to shrink our expectations. To celebrate alone. To keep our heads down and avoid asking questions that no one seems interested in answering.

But ministry cannot thrive in a vacuum. It requires context, conversation, and communal memory. When we gather students into sacred space, we are not just running a program—we are creating a moment of ecclesial life. If the broader institution doesn't absorb or reflect that life, it slowly disappears. The silence isn't just quiet. It's formative. And if we don't challenge it, it becomes the norm.

SILENCE FROM LEADERSHIP

You don't hear "no." You just don't hear anything. You submit your retreat calendar for the year. Silence. You send an idea for improving sacramental prep. Silence. You ask if the new pastoral plan has space for youth or adult formation. Silence.

Then suddenly, weeks or months later, someone asks why the event was scheduled the way it was. Or why more parents weren't involved. Or why the numbers aren't higher. You're caught off guard—not because the question is unfair, but because no one had previously indicated they were paying attention. The silence made it seem like the decisions were yours alone—until they weren't.

This kind of silence is not passive. It is formative. It trains ministers to make decisions in a vacuum and then punishes them for doing so. It creates an environment where guidance is unclear, support is minimal, and feedback arrives only after something goes wrong. The result is a culture of reactive scrutiny rather than proactive collaboration.

Many lay ministers don't want total autonomy. They want clarity. They want to know where the guardrails are, what vision their work is meant to support, and how their ministry fits into the life of the parish or school. Instead, they are often handed a vague mandate—"build community," "increase engagement," "make it more spiritual"—and then left to decipher what those phrases actually mean in practice.

Silence from leadership doesn't just leave decisions unspoken. It leaves values unarticulated. Without vision-setting or theological framing, the minister is left to intuit what matters most. Is it reverence? Is it participation? Is it evangelization through beauty or through belonging? These are not trivial distinctions. They

Institutional Silence

shape everything from how a retreat is planned to how students are invited into service. When leadership doesn't name its priorities, ministers must guess. And guessing breeds anxiety.

Sometimes the silence is logistical. A new pastor arrives but never schedules a meeting. A principal expresses general support but avoids discussing the details of liturgy or formation. Other times, the silence is strategic—an avoidance of difficult conversations, a hesitancy to commit to a vision that might stir discomfort. Either way, the result is the same: the minister operates in a fog.

And in that fog, the weight of ministry grows heavier. Because the decisions still have to be made. The emails still need to go out. The retreats still need to be planned. The calendar still needs to be filled. But with every task completed in isolation, the minister becomes more distant from the structures that were supposed to sustain them. That distance is sometimes not mere metaphor. How many parish offices have a pastoral office or a front office, and a separate building for the faith formation office?

Eventually, the silence shapes your instincts. You stop asking for feedback because none comes. You stop proposing new ideas because they vanish into the void. You stop assuming anyone will show up—not just to the event, but to you. Leadership becomes something you work around, not with. This erosion of trust is subtle. It rarely explodes into conflict. It seeps in over time. The absence of dialogue becomes the absence of shared responsibility. And without shared responsibility, the minister slowly becomes a contractor—not a collaborator.

What makes this dynamic particularly damaging is that it is often misread. To the outside observer, the minister appears independent, self-sufficient, capable. But inside, the minister is navigating uncertainty with no compass and little backup. When the silence finally breaks, it's often in the form of critique—an email forwarded from a parent, a scheduling issue blamed on miscommunication, a concern raised after the fact. And because the prior silence offered no anchor, the critique lands not as feedback, but as failure.

Part II: What They're Really Leaving

Lay ministry cannot flourish in a system where silence is the norm. Formation requires conversation. Collaboration requires visibility. If lay ministers are to serve the Church's mission with integrity, then leadership—clerical and administrative—must speak with them, not just about them. Because when leaders go silent, ministers are left listening only to their own self-doubt.

THE FOG OF RESPONSIBILITY

The job description said "faith formation." The interview said "community engagement." The day-to-day says, "Figure it out." Ministers are often brought into parishes and schools with hopeful language and enthusiastic handshakes—"We're so glad you're here," "We've needed someone like you for a long time," "Just do whatever you think will help bring people in." It sounds empowering, even liberating. But what seems like freedom is often the absence of structure. And in that absence, clarity disappears.

No one says what success looks like. No one names the priorities. No one articulates what belongs at the center of your efforts. And so you begin building—piecemeal, from instinct and borrowed models, trying to balance inherited programs with your own prayerful vision. You plan the events, write the emails, train the volunteers, and hope that s?But the direction never comes. And the more responsibility you carry, the heavier the silence becomes.

This is the fog: high expectations cloaked in low communication. You are responsible for increasing engagement, but no one defines what engagement means. You are responsible for sacramental prep, but the theological and pastoral priorities shift depending on who you ask.

In this fog, it becomes nearly impossible to lead with confidence. Every decision feels provisional. Every change feels risky. Every success feels suspect—because what if it wasn't aligned with someone's unspoken preferences? The uncertainty makes even your wins feel fragile.

Meanwhile, the institutional memory lives elsewhere. You weren't here when that tradition started. You didn't know the backstory behind that family's frustration. You didn't realize the pastor had strong feelings about that one hymn. But you're here now, and that means the blame lands with you.

There's no malice in it. Just inertia. A system that runs on assumptions: that ministry will happen, that someone will take care of it, that faith will carry on with minimal interruption. So when there's a misstep—when registration numbers drop, when a parent complains, when a Mass feels flat—it's easy for others to assume the minister dropped the ball. After all, wasn't that your job?

Responsibility without vision is a recipe for exhaustion. It demands presence without offering direction. You show up, again and again, trying to animate structures that no longer hold and programs that no longer resonate, hoping something you do will land. But in the absence of shared vision, every move feels improvisational. You become reactive, not because you lack initiative, but because you lack anchors.

This is not the same as being under-resourced, though that too is common. This is being under-communicated. It is leadership by implication. Direction by osmosis. You begin to build a ministry not from discernment but from triangulation—gauging what the school board wants, what the pastor might approve, what the parents expect, and what the students will tolerate.

In that swirl of competing expectations, you begin to disappear. Your voice, your charism, your theological imagination gets quieter. Not because you've lost your conviction—but because the fog has made it hard to know where it belongs. Ministers need direction, not micromanagement. They need shared vision, not vague affirmation. They need structures that don't just hold them accountable, but actually hold them. The fog will always be part of ministry—discernment is messy, people are unpredictable, and the Spirit resists blueprints. But that doesn't mean ministers should be left to wander. Naming the fog is the first step toward lifting it.

Part II: What They're Really Leaving

WHAT SILENCE TEACHES US TO EXPECT

You learn not to follow up. Not because you don't care, but because the last three emails were never answered. You learn not to propose new ideas. Not because you've run out of inspiration, but because the last idea died in a meeting where no one responded. You learn not to ask for help. Not because you don't need it, but because the last time you did, the help came with strings or not at all.

This is what institutional silence forms in a minister: not resentment, not outright despair—but a slow, quiet resignation. The first year you enter with energy. You have ideas. You see gaps you want to fill. You offer suggestions for revitalizing sacramental prep, deepening retreat content, or creating opportunities for student leadership. You assume people want to talk about these things—that your voice matters, that your creativity is a contribution, not a complication.

But when the meetings are short and the decisions have already been made, you start to learn the real rules. Silence becomes a teacher. And what it teaches you, again and again, is how to lower your expectations. You stop dreaming. You stop drafting. You stop pushing. You show up, do what's expected, run the events, and quietly disappear back into your office. Not out of laziness—but out of self-preservation.

This is the internal cost of ministerial silence: it doesn't just mute your voice externally. It conditions you to mute yourself internally. It rewrites your instincts. Instead of asking, "What's possible here?" you begin asking, "What will draw the least resistance?" When silence becomes the norm, initiative becomes risk. And when initiative becomes risk, ministry becomes mechanical.

You keep the schedule. You cover the bases. You do the work. But you no longer bring your whole self to the table, because the table has taught you it doesn't want the whole you. It wants compliance, not collaboration. It wants execution, not discernment. This is how good ministers begin to fade—not by leaving, but by silencing themselves before anyone else has to.

Institutional Silence

What's most disheartening is that this erosion is rarely intentional. No one sets out to make ministers feel small. No one sends a memo asking them to stop dreaming. It happens by omission. By absence. By that meeting that didn't happen, that feedback that never came, that idea that went ignored.

Over time, silence doesn't just shape your decisions—it shapes your sense of self. You start to believe that this must be what ministry is. That loneliness is part of the job. That your voice is a luxury the system can't afford.

But ministry isn't meant to be solitary. At its best, it is collaborative, discerning, Spirit-led work rooted in shared mission. And while no job is free from disappointment or miscommunication, persistent silence is not a neutral condition. It's a formative one. It shapes what ministers believe they are allowed to hope for. It trains them in defensiveness and discouragement. It tells them not to ask for more.

The challenge is to unlearn what silence teaches. To name its effects clearly. To speak, gently but persistently, where others have grown quiet. To believe that ministry should not be a solo performance but a shared journey, grounded in truth and mutual trust. Because silence may teach you to expect less—but the Gospel teaches us to expect more.

Accompaniment Meditation II

Before reading any further, take a moment to open your Bible and find the story of the road to Emmaus—Luke 24:13–35. Read it slowly. Let the story speak for itself.

ON THE ROAD WITH THE DISILLUSIONED

Two disciples walk away from Jerusalem. They are not running from scandal. They are not rebelling against teachings. They are walking home after a weekend of heartbreak. They had dared to believe that something might change—that Jesus might be the one to redeem Israel—and now, with that hope buried in a borrowed tomb, they begin the slow return to ordinary life.

Their steps are heavy. Their words, confused. And most strikingly, when the risen Christ draws near, they don't recognize Him. They're not ready to. Their grief clouds their vision. This is not just a story about two disciples. It's a mirror held up to the Church.

Many young people today walk that same road—away from the center, away from the noise, away from the expectations that once promised spiritual clarity. Not because they stopped caring. But because they once cared deeply, and now they feel betrayed or bewildered. They were told what to expect if they believed. And then something fell apart.

It's easy to look at disaffiliation and diagnose rebellion or apathy. But what if the deeper story is grief? What if the Church they hoped for hasn't shown up? What if they're not leaving the faith, but walking away from what feels like a failure to live it?

In the Emmaus story, Jesus doesn't stop them and demand they return. He walks with them. He listens first. He waits until they are ready. That kind of presence is rare—and powerful. Our job is not to drag people back to Jerusalem. Our job is to walk the road they're on—quietly, compassionately, and patiently—until their hearts begin to burn again.

THE GOD WHO WALKS BESIDE THEM

He could have stopped them. From the moment Jesus drew near on the road, He could have said, "It's me. I'm alive. Turn around." But He didn't.

Instead, He asks a question. "What are you discussing as you walk along?" He doesn't lead with proof. He doesn't lecture. He doesn't correct their theology. He listens. Even when their account is confused—even when they misinterpret the resurrection as rumor—He lets them speak. He listens long enough to understand not just what they're saying, but what they're feeling.

That moment reveals something profound about how God engages with disappointment: not by overpowering it, but by walking inside it. Too often, ministry defaults to explanation. When someone leaves or struggles, we want to respond with a program, a pamphlet, a podcast. We want to clarify the teaching, correct the misunderstanding, offer the right resources. But Jesus doesn't do any of that at first. He just walks beside them.

This is not passivity. It's presence. And it's the hardest form of ministry. Because it requires us to be comfortable with uncertainty. To stay close even when someone is venting their doubts or reliving their pain. It means letting questions hang in the air without rushing to fill them. It means holding space for someone to be lost for a while—because healing usually starts there.

The risen Christ doesn't keep His distance until they figure it out. He draws near before they even know they need Him. This is where real accompaniment begins. Not with persuasion. Not with answers. With presence. With quiet, patient nearness. With a willingness to walk as long as it takes, not to correct the person but to love them all the way through the confusion. That's what Christ did. That's what we're called to do.

RECOGNIZING HIM IN THE BREAKING

It wasn't the Scripture study on the road. It wasn't the burning in their hearts. It was the breaking of the bread. That's when their eyes were opened. We often expect transformation to happen all at once—like a sudden return to the sacraments, a dramatic testimony, or a clear commitment to discipleship. But for the disciples at Emmaus, recognition unfolded slowly. The journey itself was formation. The conversation planted seeds. The welcome at the table prepared the ground. And then, in the simplest of actions—in the breaking of bread—they saw.

Christ was known not by argument but by intimacy. Not by being convinced, but by being fed. For many young people disillusioned with the Church, what opens their eyes is not a theological proof but a human moment: being seen, being listened to, being received without agenda. And yes—being invited into the Eucharist, not as a reward for getting it all together, but as a place to meet the God who broke Himself open for them.

Conversion is rarely clean. It doesn't follow a syllabus. It can't be programmed. It comes when grace catches someone off guard and invites them back to the table. We do not control that moment. But we can walk the road that leads to it. We can make space for hearts to burn and hands to reach. We can prepare the table—trusting that Christ will make Himself known when the time is right. And when He does, it won't be because we orchestrated it. It will be because we stayed.

Accompaniment Meditation II

A PRAYER FOR THE MINISTER ON THE ROAD

Lord,

I am tired.

Tired of the silence after so much effort. Tired of the weight of walking beside others while holding my own questions. Tired of offering invitations that go unanswered, truths that go unheard.

But still—I am here.

Teach me again the way of the road.

Make me the kind of minister who walks without rushing, who listens without needing to fix, who trusts that presence is its own proclamation. Teach me how to walk with the disillusioned. Let their stories matter. Let their pain speak.

Hold me back from easy answers.

Teach me how to ask the right questions. Give me the humility to not always be the one speaking. Give me the courage to stay when they do not understand, and the grace to keep loving when they walk away.

Help me prepare the table, even when the room feels empty. Help me believe that the breaking of bread still reveals You. Let me be content with the quiet moment, the slow conversion, the grace that works unseen.

And when I doubt that anything I do matters, remind me:

You are already on the road.

I am simply catching up.

Amen.

Part III

What We're Really Called To

Chapter 8

Ministry as Accompaniment, Not Management

WE'VE NAMED THE WEIGHT of lay ministry in a disaffiliating Church. We've traced the erosion of trust, the burden of substitution, the performance traps, and the cost of control. We've seen how the same dynamics that burn out ministers also fail to form disciples. And we've listened to the silence of young people who never truly belonged. But naming the problem is only half the work. The other half—the harder half—is remembering the call.

This part of the book is not about new strategies. It's about a new way of seeing. A reorientation toward what ministry is really for—not program success, not institutional maintenance, not personal validation, but communion. Communion with one another. Communion with Christ.

These next chapters are about reclaiming the slow, relational, Spirit-led path of accompaniment. They are about letting go of the illusion that we can manage our way to transformation. They are about becoming the kind of ministers who are not just running events, but walking with souls. Because ministry doesn't begin with control. It begins with presence.

Part III: What We're Really Called To

PRESENCE OVER PROGRAMMING

Ministry doesn't happen on a schedule. It shows up in doorways and detours. It happens when someone lingers after class or stops you in the parking lot with a question they've never said out loud before. It begins with a sigh, a shrug, a silence that dares you to ask what's really going on. And if you're in a hurry—or just trying to get to the next item on your task list—you'll miss it.

The most sacred moments in ministry rarely happen during the official programming. They happen around the edges, in the margins of our neatly prepared events. A student returns to the chapel after everyone else has left. A volunteer breaks down in tears during cleanup. A parent corners you at dismissal to confess how scared they are for their child's faith. These are the unplanned encounters where the real work begins—not because they were strategic, but because you were available.

Programming, by its nature, requires control. It relies on structure and timing and execution. There's nothing inherently wrong with that—it's how we gather people, how we teach, how we host. But when programming becomes the core of ministry, it risks displacing the quiet, slow, and relational nature of spiritual growth. We start treating formation like a product to deliver instead of a relationship to nurture.

Presence is different. Presence doesn't rush. It doesn't pivot immediately to solutions. It makes space for people to be seen before they're fixed, heard before they're redirected. It slows down long enough for trust to grow—and trust is the soil where grace takes root.

Many ministers, especially those operating under tight schedules or heavy expectations, find it difficult to prioritize this kind of presence. There's always another meeting, another email, another set of chairs to stack. But the truth is: no amount of efficiency will ever substitute for a person who feels genuinely accompanied.

Presence requires margin. It demands that we hold part of ourselves back from the frenzy so that we can be truly responsive. We can't accompany others if we're always arriving late, multitasking, or already thinking about what's next. If we're too busy to notice someone's pain, we're too busy to minister.

Jesus did not build his ministry on programming. He walked. He stopped. He noticed. He asked questions and waited for answers. Even when surrounded by crowds, his attention was always deeply personal. He didn't rush to meet quotas or market impact. He focused on the person in front of him.

If we want to reclaim a more human—and more Christlike—model of ministry, we must begin by reclaiming our availability. Not in the sense of being on-call 24/7, but in the deeper sense of being attuned and interruptible. To be present is to hold space open—not just physically, but spiritually—for grace to arrive in ways we cannot predict.

There is no spreadsheet for presence. It won't make your quarterly report. But it will change lives. Because when a young person decides to open up, what they're scanning for—consciously or not—is availability. Are you paying attention? Do you have the capacity to listen? Are you really with me, or just trying to get through this? You can't fake that. They know.

This kind of ministry is costly. It means staying when you're tired. It means listening when you'd rather advise. It means choosing the person over the plan. But it's in these interruptions—these unscripted moments—that we become most like Christ.

Presence is the antidote to ministry that feels performative. It's how we remain grounded when the pressure to deliver gets loud. And it's what young people remember, long after the event ends: the adult who stayed. The conversation that didn't feel rushed. The space where they weren't just welcomed—they were heard. We don't need more programs. We need more presence.

WALKING WITH, NOT AHEAD OF

True accompaniment demands a shift—not just in method, but in posture. It's not about leading from the front or pushing from behind. It's about walking alongside, at a pace set by love, not by urgency.

Part III: What We're Really Called To

This is harder than it sounds. Ministry is often driven by momentum. There are goals to reach, benchmarks to meet, and calendars that demand movement. We are praised for initiative, evaluated on outcomes, and trained to always be one step ahead. But accompaniment doesn't fit that rhythm. It is, at its heart, a surrender of pace. It invites us to slow down, match steps, and be attentive not to where we think people should be, but to where they actually are.

To walk with someone is to honor their process. This is not over spiritualized ministry jargon. It is incarnational. Consider the wisdom from Thomas Hart's incredibly accessible work, *The Art of Christian Listening* where he reminds his readers,

> "If the church is sacramental, if human beings, in the Spirit of Jesus, are the sacrament of God's presence and action in the world, then we meet more than the person whose assistance we seek. The encounter is sacramental. It does not matter whether the helper is ordained or not, or whether the transaction is an officially acknowledged ritual sacrament or not. The invisible is somehow present in the visible."[1]

It means resisting the urge to accelerate their spiritual journey for the sake of optics or comfort. It means being present to their questions—even when the answers don't come. It means holding space for sorrow, confusion, or resistance without feeling the need to immediately redirect or resolve.

When Jesus walked with the disciples on the road to Emmaus, He did not rush them to clarity. He listened. He asked what they were talking about. He let them vent, grieve, even misunderstand. Only after walking with them in their sorrow did He begin to open the Scriptures. Even then, He waited for them to invite Him in.

That kind of patience is rare in institutional settings. Too often, we approach ministry like a tour guide: pointing out what's ahead, keeping people on schedule, and gently herding them toward the next destination. But faith doesn't grow well on tour

---

1. Hart, *Art of Christian Listening*, 9.

buses. It grows in companionship—one slow, often winding, step at a time.[2]

Accompaniment is not leadership by coercion. It's not discipleship by acceleration. It's a mutual recognition of dignity: I will not leave you behind, and I will not drag you forward. I will walk with you, even if the path is unclear and the progress slow.

This kind of humility can be unsettling. It forces us to give up the illusion of control. It asks us to abandon our timelines and let the Holy Spirit lead. Sometimes, it even means admitting we don't know where this is going—but we're committed to walking it together anyway.

There is a deep trust required here. Trust that God is already at work in the person beside us. Trust that our role is not to engineer their conversion, but to be a witness to it. Trust that slowness is not failure, and that questions are not threats. We don't accompany to produce results. We accompany because Christ does.

When we walk ahead of people, we risk losing them. When we walk behind, we risk resenting them. Or them resenting us. But when we walk with them—really with them—we begin to rediscover the heart of ministry. Not as task completion, but as communion. We don't need to be out front to lead. We just need to be faithful enough to stay beside.

RECLAIMING THE PASTORAL HEART

Ministry has always been a human endeavor—rooted in presence, relationship, and the messy, beautiful work of shepherding souls. But somewhere along the way, we've absorbed a different rhythm: one shaped by productivity, not presence. We now find ourselves expected to run ministries like programs, execute plans like projects, and deliver results like vendors. The pastoral heart is still beating, but it is muffled under the noise of metrics, scheduling tools, and institutional demands.

---

2. USCCB, *Listen, Teach, Send*, 53–54.

Part III: What We're Really Called To

To reclaim the pastoral heart is to remember what ministry is actually for. It is not meant to be a series of transactions—event for attendance, volunteer for service hours, sacrament for registration fee. It is meant to be deeply incarnational: rooted in flesh-and-blood encounters, in lives shared, and in the slow work of grace unfolding in real time.

Too often, lay ministers are handed the sacred responsibility of accompaniment but pressured to execute it through a corporate lens. We are asked to demonstrate success in ways that are easily packaged: attendance growth, social media presence, parent satisfaction. These aren't inherently bad—but when they become the primary measure of health, we lose something essential.

Because the pastoral heart doesn't always produce visible fruit. Sometimes it just sits beside a grieving parent. Sometimes it listens to the same student wrestle with the same doubt for the third time in a month. Sometimes it sends a text, makes a phone call, lights a candle. These things don't go on spreadsheets—but they are the heartbeat of ministry.

Reclaiming that heart means re-centering on presence over programming. It means giving ministers the room to be human—and to meet others in their humanity. It means shifting away from a transactional model of Church, where ministry is measured by delivery and response, and moving toward a shared journey of discipleship where no one is left alone.

When the pastoral heart is honored, ministry begins to breathe again. Events become encounters. Meetings become moments of discernment. Check-ins become confessions of the soul. And ministers themselves begin to heal—not by doing less, but by doing what they were actually called to do: love with their whole selves.

This isn't a romanticism of ministry. It's a reclamation of its essence. Because people are not problems to be solved. They are lives to be shared. And if we forget that, we've forgotten why we began.

Chapter 9

Giving Away the Keys

YOU DON'T HAVE TO DO IT ALL

SOMEWHERE ALONG THE WAY, many lay ministers begin to internalize a dangerous belief: if something is going to get done—and get done right—it has to be done by them. It doesn't start that way. Most of us enter ministry with a collaborative spirit and a desire to serve. But after enough no-shows, enough last-minute cancellations, enough blank stares in planning meetings, the instinct to do it alone starts to take hold. It feels easier. Cleaner. More efficient. And for a while, it works.

The deeper cost, however, is harder to name. It's not just exhaustion, though that inevitably comes. It's the stifling of potential in those around you. When you carry the full weight of ministry on your back, you rob others of the chance to carry part of it with you. What could have been a moment of formation becomes a transaction. What could have been leadership becomes logistics. And what could have been a community becomes an audience. Delegation is not a compromise of fidelity. It is a practice of trust. And trust is at the heart of ministry.

Jesus did not multiply His mission by doing everything Himself. He formed disciples. He sent them out, sometimes before they were fully ready.[1] He gave them real authority, not just tasks. He corrected them, yes, but He never micromanaged their faithfulness. When they failed—and they did—He stayed close. When they succeeded, He rejoiced. That is what trust looks like in ministry: not abandonment of responsibility, but a willingness to share it.

To give others space to lead, we must confront our own ego. Sometimes we're afraid that if someone else does it, it won't be as good. Sometimes we're afraid that if someone else does it well, we won't be needed. Both fears are rooted in the same lie: that our value comes from being indispensable. It doesn't. Our value comes from being faithful.

When a student leads prayer for the first time, or a parent takes ownership of an event, or a colleague steps into planning with fresh vision—that's not a threat. It's fruit. The truth is, you don't have to do it all. You're not supposed to. Ministry done alone is ministry that burns out. Ministry shared is ministry that endures.

The call to "give away the keys" starts here: with the inner work of releasing the illusion that everything depends on you. It doesn't. It depends on Christ—and His Church is bigger than your calendar. So no, you do not have to do it all alone. You might hear that good news and acknowledge it, but until you internalize it, and until those around you are formed to lift the weight with you, your ministry will be exhausting.

TRUSTING THE INEXPERIENCED

At some point in every ministry setting, someone will ask, "But are they ready?" It usually comes in response to a new volunteer, a student given a leadership role, or someone stepping into a visible responsibility for the first time. The question isn't wrong. Discernment matters. But often, the deeper concern beneath it isn't readiness—it's control.

If we only ever trust people once they've proven themselves, we've missed the point of formation. Formation means giving

---

1. Luke 10:1–72.

people space to grow while they lead—not just after they've arrived. It means allowing mistakes, guiding through them, and resisting the urge to reclaim the reins every time the process gets messy.

Jesus didn't wait until the disciples were perfectly formed before sending them out. He sent them two by two while they were still learning.[2] He entrusted them with healing, teaching, and proclaiming the Kingdom—even though they misunderstood Him, argued among themselves, and asked the wrong questions. Their call didn't wait for their perfection. It preceded it.

In contemporary ministry, we often treat leadership like a prize for good behavior or advanced knowledge. But real leadership formation doesn't happen in the classroom. It happens in the field. Students don't learn how to pray out loud until we ask them to. Volunteers don't gain confidence until they've stumbled and found their voice. Formation is participatory, not passive. You don't get good at leadership by watching someone else do it. You get good by doing—imperfectly, awkwardly, courageously.

And yet, many ministers hesitate. We've been burned before. The student flaked. The parent overstepped. The young adult made it about themselves. So we retreat. We tell ourselves it's better to wait until they're ready. But what we often mean is until it's safe. And ministry—true formation—is never entirely safe. It's vulnerable. It requires surrender. And it trusts that the Holy Spirit is doing work in them we can't fully see.

Some of the most transformative leaders I've worked with started with no qualifications except a willing heart. They were shy, unsure, inconsistent. But someone believed in them. And that belief created space for the Spirit to move.

To trust the inexperienced is not to abandon standards. It is to recognize that standards alone don't make saints. Faith does. It changes how people see themselves. It calls forth courage. It invites grace to grow.

The work of the minister, then, is not just to hold space for success—but to hold space for growth. To let the liturgical reader stumble through their first reading. To let the retreat leader forget

---

2. Luke 10:1–12

their place in the schedule. To let the small group facilitator ask a clumsy question. And then, to walk with them afterward—not in judgment, but in honest reflection, encouragement, and another opportunity. This kind of accompaniment is slow. It's inefficient. It won't always look polished. But it is the soil of real transformation.

Because when we entrust others before they feel ready, we're not only reflecting Christ's model—we're announcing a deeper truth: that God doesn't call the qualified. He qualifies the called.

FROM RECRUITMENT TO RELATIONSHIP

It's easy to slip into the rhythm of recruitment: we need a lector, a small group leader, someone to run music or set up chairs. Ministry gets busy, events stack up, and before long, the default strategy is filling roles. Who's available? Who's willing? Who can we ask to do it—again? But people aren't puzzle pieces. They don't exist to complete our spreadsheets or solve our logistical gaps. And when ministry begins to treat them that way—however unintentionally—it stops being relational. It becomes transactional.

We don't mean to do it. Most ministers are deeply pastoral. But we're also under pressure. We're told to staff events, grow attendance, and prove engagement. That pressure nudges us toward quick asks and short-term solutions. A sign-up sheet replaces a conversation. A text replaces prayerful discernment. The need becomes more urgent than the person we're asking to meet it.

The result? Volunteers feel like cogs, not co-laborers. Students feel used, not seen. And ministers begin to confuse availability with formation—assuming that because someone showed up to help, they've been led.

Real empowerment doesn't start with asking, "What can you do?" It starts with asking, "Who are you becoming?" It begins in relationship: knowing someone's story, understanding their strengths, recognizing their fears, and walking with them long before and long after they step into a leadership role. It's the difference between recruitment and accompaniment.

Jesus didn't recruit His disciples like workers for a project. He called them into relationship. He spent time with them. He asked questions. He let them follow, fail, and try again. He didn't fill roles—He formed people. Even when they misunderstood Him, even when they weren't ready, He stayed close. He invited them not just to do ministry, but to become ministers of the Kingdom.

When ministry flows from that posture, everything changes. A student becomes more than a retreat leader—they become a steward of grace in their community. A volunteer becomes more than someone who sets up tables—they become a bearer of hospitality and belonging. Tasks are no longer the endpoint. They're part of the larger journey of discipleship.

And yes, this kind of ministry is slower. It doesn't guarantee polished outcomes. It means having more one-on-one conversations, more spiritual mentoring, more patient walking. But it also means deeper roots. Stronger ownership. Lasting transformation.

The temptation will always be to slide back into recruitment. Especially when numbers are low, when deadlines loom, when the same five people keep stepping up. But the task of ministry is not to keep the machine running. It's to form people in Christ. And that begins with relationship.

So ask the next person not just if they can help—but how they're doing. Ask what's on their heart. Ask what lights them up. Ask what they're afraid to say yes to. And then, listen. Walk with them. Let your ministry begin there. Because when we shift from recruitment to relationship, we stop filling roles—and start forming disciples.

LETTING GO WITHOUT CHECKING OUT

One of the great misunderstandings in ministry is that empowering others means stepping away entirely. That to trust someone with leadership, we have to vacate the space ourselves. But letting go of control doesn't mean vanishing—it means showing up differently.

Part III: What We're Really Called To

Ministry isn't a relay race where we pass the baton and walk off the track. It's a pilgrimage. There are moments when others lead, moments when we walk beside, and moments when we quietly fall back to let them discover their own pace. But we're always still on the road.

This is where many well-meaning ministers struggle. We know we need to delegate. We believe in student ownership, parish collaboration, shared leadership. But in practice, we often oscillate between over-functioning and total withdrawal. We either grip the reins tightly—afraid it will all fall apart without us—or we throw them off completely, hoping delegation will resolve our exhaustion. Neither posture works. Both breed resentment.

We learned this habit from our pastors. Too many lay ministers were given programs to run without mentorship, trust, or accompaniment—just a vague blessing and the expectation to figure it out. We were handed keys, not community. And after a few years of surviving under that kind of leadership, we began to imitate it ourselves. We delegate without presence. We empower without walking alongside. We expect students or volunteers to rise to the occasion alone—just like we had to. But that's not empowerment. That's repetition. And the result is a ministry culture where everyone feels a little bit abandoned, even as the language of leadership keeps circulating.

True accompaniment means staying close, even when we're no longer the central figure. It means attending a student-led retreat not to critique or hover, but simply to be present. It means letting a volunteer team plan a liturgy while trusting that your quiet presence at the back of the room still matters. It means answering the late-night text without rushing to solve everything. It means remaining faithful without being in control.

In the Gospels, Jesus models this kind of letting go with remarkable care. He sends His disciples out in pairs—not alone. He gives them real authority but also clear guidance. He lets them try, fail, come back, and try again. And when they falter, He doesn't withdraw His trust. He draws closer. Think of Peter after the denial, restored not with a lecture but with breakfast and three quiet questions: Do you love me?[3]

This is the difference between abandonment and accompaniment. One leaves people to sink or swim. The other watches from the shore, ready to wade in if needed, but confident that growth happens in the going.

When ministers disappear after delegating, young leaders notice. They internalize the message that responsibility comes with isolation, or that their efforts aren't worth sustained support. But when we remain near—prayerful, available, invested—we show them that leadership is not a test to pass but a relationship to be held. That they are not alone in the work. That we believe in them even before they believe in themselves.

Letting go, then, is not a retreat from ministry. It is a shift in posture—from doing to being, from directing to discipling. It is about walking with those we've empowered, not because we doubt them, but because that's what love does.

You don't have to run every meeting. You don't have to plan every event. But your presence, even in the background, speaks volumes. It says: I see you. I trust you. I'm still here. And sometimes, that's what makes the difference.

A MINISTRY THAT MULTIPLIES

If ministry depends on one person's talent, charisma, or endurance, it will not last. But if it becomes a space where others are empowered, trusted, and formed—it multiplies. This is the long game of lay ministry: not managing programs, but forming people who can carry the mission forward. It means shifting from ownership to stewardship, from guarding our methods to investing in others' callings. Multiplication isn't about numbers—it's about legacy.

The measure of faithfulness isn't how much we accomplish ourselves, but how many others we lift into responsibility, discernment, and mission. We are not building monuments to our own

---

3. John 21:14–16

Part III: What We're Really Called To

vision. We are building communities that can thrive after we've moved on. And that begins when we give away what was never ours to hoard: responsibility, leadership, trust.

This chapter began with the fear that delegation might mean dilution. But what we find instead is that when we entrust others with the work, we don't lose impact—we multiply it. Not by control, but by communion. The Church doesn't need more solo leaders. It needs people willing to form others who can lead. Ministry that multiplies is slow. It's relational. It's messy. But it lasts.

Chapter 10

You Can't Program Formation

THE ILLUSION OF THE BIG EVENT

WE'VE ALL SEEN IT—THE high-energy retreat, the emotional keynote, the dramatic moment in adoration of the Blessed Sacrament. The kind of moment that seems to change everything. Students are crying. Volunteers are praying over one another. The Spirit feels palpable in the room. And for a brief moment, it seems like this one event will be the turning point.

But then Monday comes. And the students return to class. The volunteers go back to their routines. The retreat is over, and with it, much of what seemed so real in the moment quietly slips away.

In ministry, we've built an entire culture around these peak experiences. We measure their success by the emotional height of the evening or the number of students who raise their hands in response.[1] We spend months planning logistics, printing T-shirts, designing stage backdrops, crafting the perfect playlist. And none of those things are wrong—many of them can be useful. The problem is that we've begun to confuse the moment for the movement.

---

1. Interestingly enough, perhaps unknowingly, ministries who emphasize the mountaintop "retreat high" without the foundational work of continuously coming to God in prayer and the Sacraments, can be seen as the ancient Christian heresy of Messalainism, where the presence of the Holy Spirit in one's life was believed to be measured by emotional experiences.

Part III: What We're Really Called To

We treat the event as the engine of conversion, when at best, it's the spark.

The Christian life was never meant to be sustained by mountaintop moments. Even Jesus, after the Transfiguration, walked back down into the valley. The pattern of discipleship is not one of constant elevation, but of continual return—return to prayer, return to the sacraments, return to community, return to Christ. Formation happens in the repetition.

It's much easier to capture the joy of a retreat than the quiet discipline of a student showing up for Mass each Sunday. It's easier to rally excitement for a conference than to invite someone to a regular small group. It's easier to fundraise for a one-time mission trip than to invest in year-round spiritual mentorship. And yet, it's the latter that actually forms disciples.

The illusion of the big event is that it can carry the weight of ongoing formation. It can't. Not because the events are meaningless, but because they are incomplete. They are moments of encounter, not ecosystems of growth. Make no mistake, these initial moments of encounter with the risen Lord are vital to the development of faith in an individual. However, without habits to anchor what was experienced, even the most powerful event dissolves into memory.

Too often, our ministry calendars are filled with one-off events stacked back-to-back, each designed to be an on-ramp to deeper faith. But if there's no clear road to continue on, the on-ramp leads nowhere. Students show up, have an experience, and then drift—because no one helped them take the next step. No one taught them how to build a life of faith, not just a weekend of it.

This is not a critique of big events. Many of us can name a retreat or a youth conference that genuinely changed our lives. But even those moments only bore fruit because they were followed by something more—someone who followed up, a space to pray, a habit that formed.

Events matter. But they must be nested in a larger rhythm of formation. If ministry becomes a series of disconnected highs, it produces emotional dependence, not spiritual maturity. It leaves people chasing the next mountaintop, instead of learning how to walk with God through the plains and valleys of life.[2] Real faith isn't built on the highlight reel. It's built in the hidden hours. So yes, hold the retreat. Host the speaker. Run the event. But don't mistake it for the work. The work is what happens after.

THE DAILY WORK OF DISCIPLESHIP

Discipleship is not a breakthrough—it's a practice. And like all meaningful practices, it grows through repetition. This is perhaps the greatest disconnect between how many ministries are structured and how actual formation unfolds. While our calendars are built around moments of impact, the soul matures in the quiet, ordinary disciplines of faithfulness.

There's nothing flashy about showing up to daily Mass. There's no applause for opening the Scriptures in your room and reading a chapter slowly. No one posts pictures of a teenager choosing to pray the Liturgy of the Hours alone. But these are the habits that shape saints.

We live in a culture that rewards novelty and visibility. A student who gives a witness talk or serves on retreat is easily praised. But the same student, choosing to go to confession regularly or silently fasting on Fridays, is usually unnoticed. That's not a criticism of celebration—it's a reminder that celebration alone doesn't sustain formation. Formation is slow, embodied, and deeply personal. It's built over time, not in a single experience.

Too often, we've handed young people opportunities to perform before we've taught them how to persevere. We elevate them as leaders without helping them become disciples. The result is often burnout, confusion, or a sense of inadequacy when the emotional rush of the event fades. They assume something is wrong with them, when in fact they were never given the daily tools of the spiritual life.

---

2. Consider the Psalms of lament like Psalm 22 and 88 for deep spiritual pain while still walking with God through whatever may come.

PART III: WHAT WE'RE REALLY CALLED TO

Those tools are simple. But they are not easy. Daily prayer. Regular sacraments. Honest conversations. Acts of service. Scripture. Silence. Community. Accountability. These are not revolutionary practices, but they are transformative. They shape the heart slowly, bending it toward the love of God not in sudden flashes, but in long, steady arcs.

And they require accompaniment. A student is far more likely to commit to these practices if someone walks with them—someone who checks in, encourages them, reminds them it's okay to falter. Formation happens in relationship, not in isolation. A young person might be drawn to Christ in a moment, but they are formed in Christ by the people who surround them afterward.

This is why accountability matters—not as surveillance, but as solidarity. It's not about asking "Did you pray today?" It's about being the person who says, "Let's pray together," or "I've missed this too. Let's start again." The Christian life is a shared journey, and we can't expect students to walk it alone.

In ministry, we sometimes fear that sustained formation is boring. Even if the thought is never conscious. That we'll lose their interest if we don't constantly innovate. But the truth is, young people are starved for meaning. They're looking for something sturdy to stand on. What we think is boring might be the very structure they've been missing.

We don't need to make the Gospel entertaining. We need to make it livable. That begins with showing them how to pray, not just that they should. With building rhythms of worship, not just moments of praise. With teaching them how to endure, not just how to perform. The work of discipleship is daily.

WHY PROGRAMS CAN'T FORM SOULS

The modern parish or school often operates with an unspoken assumption: if we run the right programs, formation will follow. We build calendars, develop themes, create flyers, and evaluate attendance, believing that well-executed programming leads to

You Can't Program Formation

well-formed disciples. But the soul doesn't move on a semester schedule.

Programs are helpful. They create structure. They offer opportunities for encounter, consistency, and shared experience. But programs are not formation. They are tools—containers. What matters is what's inside them.

Too often, the container is polished while the content is hollow. We host confirmation nights that are tightly run but spiritually thin. We hold service events where students are physically present but spiritually disengaged. We celebrate youth Masses that hit all the right notes but never invite the heart to change. The programming succeeds, but the soul remains untouched.

This is not an issue of effort or intention. Most ministers work tirelessly to offer the best they can. But the structure itself can become self-referential: it exists to sustain the appearance of ministry rather than its essence. We measure faith formation by completion of requirements rather than growth in virtue. We assume participation equals transformation. It doesn't.

True formation is slow, relational, and deeply personal. It requires time, conversation, prayer, and trust. These things can't be scripted. They can't be standardized. You can't plug them into a spreadsheet. And because they don't show up easily in quarterly reports, they are often undervalued—even by those who long for them.

Students know when something is for them and when something is about them. They can tell when a retreat is planned around real needs versus when it's scheduled out of obligation. They feel the difference between a program that listens and one that lectures. When programming becomes mechanical, they check out—not because they don't care about their faith, but because they sense the experience isn't rooted in it.

Programs also struggle to adapt. Real human formation is messy. It doesn't follow timelines. Someone may have a conversion moment a year after their confirmation class ends. Someone else may ask the deepest question five minutes after an event is over. A program-driven mindset moves on. Formation doesn't.

PART III: WHAT WE'RE REALLY CALLED TO

This is where rooted community matters. Souls are not formed in classrooms or event centers—they are formed in relationships. In friendships. In mentorship. In the ordinary companionship of people who walk the road together. A community of disciples can hold someone long after the program ends. It can answer late-night doubts. It can remind someone of their dignity when they forget it themselves.

And formation also requires spiritual discipline. A student can attend six events in a semester and still be spiritually stagnant if they aren't practicing prayer, reflection, and service in daily life. Programs can point to those practices, but they can't replace them. They are scaffolding, not foundation.

None of this is to say that programs are bad. It's to say that they are insufficient on their own. We should keep running retreats. We should offer youth nights and Bible studies and mission trips. But we should never believe that those programs, by themselves, are what make disciples.

The real work is slower, quieter, and far more enduring. It happens in the in-between spaces. The check-in after school. The prayer before lunch. The invitation to serve even when no one is watching. Programs may plant the seed. But it is relationship, discipline, and grace that make it grow.

BUILDING RHYTHMS, NOT EVENTS

The event calendar cannot carry the weight of formation. For too long, we've relied on a string of high-energy, high-attendance events to keep our ministries alive: the fall retreat, the Christmas party, the Lenten mission, the summer trip. These moments can be meaningful. They may even spark something real. But they are not enough.

What forms a soul is not the momentary encounter—it's the pattern of life that surrounds it. What sustains faith over time is rhythm: daily, weekly, and seasonal practices that root a person in prayer, presence, and service. Without these rhythms, even the

You Can't Program Formation

best events collapse under their own weight. They provide transformation that the rest of the structure can't support.

We know this instinctively. Ask anyone who's led a powerful retreat and they'll describe the same tension: the mountaintop experience followed by the valley of ordinary time. The retreat "high". Students come home filled with zeal, conviction, or hope—only to find no support for that spark in their daily environment. The retreat did its job. The community didn't.

Yet, ordinary time in our Liturgical Calendar is deeply prayerful. Ministry must be reoriented around rhythms that last. This doesn't mean doing away with events. It means reframing them as milestones within a larger, ongoing journey. The real work is teaching students to pray when no one is watching, to reflect on their day with honesty, to show up for one another in small ways, over time.

One-off events are like flashlights in a dark room. They offer sudden clarity, but the room stays lit only while the batteries last. Rhythms are like windows. They let in natural light, day after day. You don't always notice the light shifting—but over time, it changes how you see.

These rhythms don't have to be complex. They can be as simple as beginning every meeting with five minutes of silence. Ending every class with a moment of gratitude. Asking one reflective question a week. Making space each month for communal service. Setting aside a consistent time for Eucharistic adoration, or Scripture study, or shared prayer. The power is not in their novelty. It's in their constancy.

This shift also redefines what ministry "success" looks like. Instead of counting heads at an event, we begin to ask: Are they learning to pray? Are they forming spiritual friendships? Are they discovering how to serve without being seen? These are slower metrics. But they are the ones that last. Business managers are rolling their eyes at this thought. Immeasurable anecdotes like these are more difficult report to the pastoral council. But paired with the attendance statistics, they begin to tell a fuller story.

Part III: What We're Really Called To

Building rhythms also requires formation for the ministers themselves. If we do not live in spiritual rhythm, we will always default to busyness. If we do not pray, we will plan instead. If we do not rest, we will overfunction. The culture of event-driven ministry is not just exhausting—it's deforming. It shapes leaders who run excellent programs but lose touch with the hearts. He w Gospel.

Jesus did not build a ministry of events. He walked, taught, prayed, rested, and broke bread—with rhythm. His formation of the disciples was not based on a calendar of strategic initiatives. It was rooted in daily life, shared meals, repeated teachings, and patient accompaniment. He created a pattern they could live out, not just remember.

If we want our ministry to form disciples, we need to build structures that support repetition. Not mindless repetition, but holy habit. Not obligation, but invitation. A way of life that slowly takes root in a person's soul and reshapes their days. Rhythms are quiet. They don't always photograph well. They're not designed for hype. But they are what hold when everything else fades.

Chapter 11

Burned Out or Burning Bright?

WHAT BURNOUT ACTUALLY LOOKS LIKE

You don't always notice burnout as it happens. It's not usually a dramatic exit or a middle-of-the-night breakdown. More often, it's a quiet recalibration of the heart—toward smaller expectations, fewer risks, and just enough energy to get through the week. It's the slow shift from ministry as a vocation to ministry as a job. You still show up. You still plan. You still respond to emails. But something in you has gone silent.

Burnout doesn't always mean you stop caring. Sometimes, it means you care so deeply, and for so long, that your heart starts shielding itself. You begin to flinch before the disappointment comes. You start pre-editing your ideas before you share them, assuming they'll be dismissed. You stop asking for help because the silence last time was louder than any refusal. You shrink—not because your love for ministry has died, but because your hope that it can flourish has worn thin.

You begin saying things like, "Let's just get through this," or "This is fine enough." And maybe it is fine enough. But fine enough is not the fire you used to carry. It's not the same as conviction. It's not the same as joy.

Part III: What We're Really Called To

There's a version of burnout that no one talks about: when your external ministry stays intact, but your internal imagination has gone quiet. You keep the machine running, but it's powered by habit, not hope. You say the right things, pray the right prayers, post the right photos—but you're not looking for grace anymore. You're looking for your next day off.

In these moments, you may still be viewed as successful. You might even be praised for your consistency. No one sees how much of your soul is being left behind.

Because real burnout is not just fatigue. It's disorientation. It's the moment you stop asking what God wants and start asking only what people need. It's when you lose the sense that you're co-laboring with Christ and start feeling like the only one holding the pieces together.[1]

You don't walk away—you can't. This is your job. This is your calling. This is the place you've poured your heart into. So instead, you shut off certain rooms inside yourself and work from what's left. Some days, you can't even name what's missing. It's not just energy. It's presence. It's the deep belief that God is still doing something here. That you're part of it. That it matters.

You can't manufacture that belief. You can't force it with more caffeine or a better planner. You need rest—not just sleep, but rest of the soul. A moment to remember that you are not the vine, only a branch. Burnout isn't always the flame going out. Sometimes it's the wick running low, flickering in a draft of indifference, trying to remember what it felt like to burn for something real.

THE ILLUSION OF THE HERO MINISTER

There's a quiet script in ministry culture that celebrates the minister who never stops. The one who always says yes. The one who stays late, picks up the slack, cancels their plans for the sake of the parish or school. We call it dedication. We call it servant leadership.

---

1. 1 Corinthians 3:9

But at some point, it stops being faithfulness and starts becoming something else—a kind of spiritualized self-erasure.

The "hero minister" narrative is subtle but powerful. It's the unspoken admiration we give to those who seem tireless, the ones who carry every program on their back and still smile through it. It's the praise of someone who "gives everything" to the Church—as if burnout were a badge of holiness.

But hidden beneath the applause is a dangerous theology: that exhaustion equals sanctity, that the more invisible your suffering, the more sacred your work. We begin to believe that saying no is selfish, setting boundaries is unspiritual, and asking for help is weakness. This isn't maturity. Calling a spade a spade, it is pride masquerading as martyrdom.

Christ gave everything—but He also withdrew to pray, took naps in boats, and said no to the crowds. He didn't heal every person. He remained rooted in the will of the Father, not in the demands of the people. The Church needs ministers who are whole—who lead from a place of communion, not depletion.

And yet, this illusion persists. We reward overfunctioning with more responsibility. We fill the calendar and call it mission. We see someone burning out and think, "They're just passionate."

There's also a form of pride that attaches itself to this illusion. We begin to believe that things will fall apart without us. That if we don't do it, no one will. And maybe that's sometimes true—but it doesn't mean we're called to carry it all. It means the structure needs fixing, not that we need to become superhuman.

This mindset isolates us. It keeps us from forming teams, mentoring others, or building sustainable rhythms. It makes ministry look impossible to the next generation—because who would want to inherit that weight? When we confuse overworking with sainthood, we stop asking what kind of fruit our work is producing. We start measuring our worth by our weariness.

True maturity in ministry isn't about doing more. It's about discerning what's yours to carry—and what's not. It's about trusting that the Kingdom of God is bigger than your capacity. It's about stepping back when needed, not to abandon the mission, but to stay faithful to it.

The illusion of the hero minister is compelling. It feels noble. Maybe even holy. But it often ends with resentment, disconnection, and burnout disguised as endurance. We don't need to be heroes. We need to be disciples—present, discerning, honest, and willing to lead in a way that doesn't destroy us.

RELEARNING HOW TO REST

Ministry often trains us to feel guilty for resting. There's always one more email to send, one more meeting to prepare, one more student to follow up with. And when the work is tied to salvation—our own or someone else's—rest can feel like negligence. How can I pause when the stakes are so high? But this is where we need to be re-formed.

Rest is not the opposite of ministry. It's a part of it. The God who called us to serve is the same God who rested on the seventh day. The same Christ who said "Come to me, all who labor"[2] also went away from the crowds to pray, to sleep, to be alone.[3] Rest isn't laziness. It's trust.

When we refuse to rest, what we're often saying—without meaning to—is that the work depends entirely on us. That if we stop, the mission stops. But ministry was never ours to sustain alone. The Holy Spirit is the one who transforms hearts, not us. The Kingdom will come, whether or not we skip lunch to finish a bulletin announcement.

Relearning how to rest requires spiritual discipline. It's not just time off—it's a posture of surrender. Can I step away, even when the work feels unfinished? Can I turn off the phone, even when someone might need something? Can I go home on time, even when there's pressure to stay?

---

2. Matthew 27:28
3. Matthew 4, 8:23–25, 26:36.

Rest exposes our idols. If we've come to believe that our worth is tied to our productivity, rest will feel like failure. If we believe that God's favor is tied to our output, rest will feel like sin. But it is neither. It is an act of faith that says: "God, I trust You more than I trust myself." Sabbath isn't just for God—it's for us. It reminds us that we are not machines, not messiahs, not irreplaceable. We are beloved sons and daughters, called to abide before we act.

In the long arc of ministry, burnout isn't a badge of honor. It's often a warning sign that we've stopped trusting God to carry what only He can carry. If we want to last, to love well, to model something livable for those we serve, we have to practice rest—not just as recovery, but as resistance. Resistance to the culture of hustle, the illusion of control, and the lie that we are only as valuable as what we produce. Relearning how to rest is relearning how to be held. It is ministry, too.

BRIGHT, NOT BURNED

There's a kind of tiredness that's holy. The kind that comes from walking with people through hard seasons, staying late to hear a student's story, or driving home after a retreat that finally broke through. It's not the kind of fatigue that crushes your spirit. It's the kind that says, "This mattered."

Ministry will wear you out. That's not a failure. The question is what kind of fire is consuming you. Are you being burned up by the demands of a system that never slows down, or are you being lit from within by a purpose that keeps you steady through it?

Too many lay ministers burn out because they're trying to match the pace and polish of an institutional machine that never rests. They're running programs, answering emails, troubleshooting logistics, and keeping everything afloat—often without meaningful support or space to reflect. The exhaustion that follows isn't just physical. It's existential. You don't just need a nap—you start to question why you said yes in the first place.

Part III: What We're Really Called To

But not all fire destroys.[4] Think of Moses and the burning bush—flames that lit up but did not consume.[5] Or the apostles at Pentecost, flames resting on their heads, not to incinerate them but to empower them.[6] Or Christ Himself, who emptied Himself in love but was never emptied of love.[7]

The call is not to avoid all exhaustion. The call is to be consumed by the right things. By compassion. By fidelity. By the quiet conviction that even when no one sees, the Kingdom is still growing.

There will be seasons where you are deeply tired—but still rooted. Still joyful. Still faithful. That's what it means to burn bright instead of burning out. To be a minister whose fire comes from within, from communion with Christ, not from running harder than the system asks.

Let your exhaustion point you toward what matters. Let it draw you back to Christ. And let it teach you that sustainable ministry doesn't mean coasting through untouched—it means burning with purpose, grounded in love, fed by grace, and never mistaking busyness for mission.

---

4. Isaiah 6:6-9 is a beautiful allegory for the Eucharist.
5. Exodus 3
6. Acts 2:1-13
7. Luke 23:39-43

Conclusion
Still Here

BEARING THE WEIGHT TOGETHER

MOST DAYS, YOU DON'T see them. They don't make headlines. They aren't speaking at conferences. They're not leading national initiatives or rebranding parish life. But they're there. Lay ministers in parishes, schools, and campuses across the country—opening doors, leading retreats, staying late to clean up after events, returning emails after dinner, walking students to the chapel, showing up even when the system is strained. They're the quiet backbone of the Church's day-to-day life. They are, in a word, still here.

And while their names may not be known beyond their corner of ministry, they are known to one another. There is a kind of quiet solidarity that exists among those who carry this weight. It shows up in hallway glances between staff who've both had long weeks. It lives in the side conversations after diocesan events, the group texts that ask for prayers and offer memes in the same swipe. It's in the unspoken understanding that the work is hard, but we're not alone in it.

For many of us, ministry has often felt isolating. The structures don't always support us. The expectations are heavy. The recognition is rare. But what keeps us from collapsing under it is the knowledge—sometimes just the faint hope—that someone else is out there, holding the line too.

Part III: What We're Really Called To

Maybe you've never met them. Maybe you've only heard their voice on a podcast or seen a glimpse of their parish bulletin online. Maybe they're a neighboring youth minister, a theology teacher across the diocese, a friend-of-a-friend whose retreat theme you borrowed once. Maybe you've never spoken—but you can feel less alone knowing they exist.

That invisible web of solidarity matters. It's not built on strategy or structure. It's built on faithfulness. On the decision to keep showing up, even when the fruit is slow and the support is minimal. It's built on a shared love for the Church—not the brand, not the bureaucracy, but the Body of Christ, messy and miraculous as it is.

There's deep strength in that kind of communion. Not the flashy kind, but the kind that holds you steady when everything else feels uncertain. The kind that reminds you your labor is not in vain. The kind that says: I see you. I'm with you. We're still here.

LETTING THE OLD MODELS DIE

Some parts of ministry need to be mourned. Not because they were bad, but because they no longer fit the landscape we now inhabit. The days of packed youth nights just because there was nothing better to do—the golden era when students would sign up for retreats en masse or parishes ran with a deep bench of committed volunteers—those days are gone in many places. And they may not come back. There's grief in naming that.

We do harm when we refuse to acknowledge that change. When we measure today's ministry by yesterday's expectations, we end up frustrated, ashamed, or quietly bitter. We begin chasing ghosts—trying to recreate a spirit that belonged to a different moment, different culture, different Church. But the longer we try to keep old models alive, the more we risk missing what the Holy Spirit is actually doing here and now.

Letting something die doesn't mean it wasn't good. It means it has served its season. What's needed now isn't a polished revival of the past—it's a re-rooting in the present. What are the needs of this moment? Where is the hunger today? Who is showing up—and what are they showing up for?

The temptation to double down on what used to work is real. If we just had more money. If the pastor was just more charismatic. If families came every Sunday. If students cared more. But if we're always working from an "if only" framework, we'll never see clearly what's possible. Worse, we'll miss what's already happening—slow, small, unseen but real.

New models of ministry won't come from strategy documents or diocesan plans alone. They'll come from ministers on the ground who are willing to adapt, to trust the process of death and resurrection. Who are willing to let something go so that something more honest, more sustainable, more Spirit-led can take its place.

Sometimes faithfulness means keeping a ministry alive. But sometimes, faithfulness means letting it go. Not every retreat needs to be saved. Not every committee needs to be staffed. Not every program needs to be defended. We are not here to prove that a legacy model can still function. We are here to witness to the living Christ in whatever shape that takes now.

The Gospel isn't dying. But some of our inherited structures are. And maybe they need to. Maybe we've been entrusted not just with their preservation, but with their burial—and with the sacred work of planting something new.

THE QUIET REVOLUTION

If you're waiting for a formal invitation to lead differently, it may never come. Most revolutions don't start from the top. They begin in quiet corners—among people who are tired of pretending everything's fine. Among people who are still showing up, but can't keep doing it the old way. Among people who trust the Gospel enough to let it disrupt even the expectations of their job description.

Lay ministry is changing. Not because someone declared it so, but because the ground itself is shifting. And in this movement, change doesn't look like rebellion. It looks like fidelity. It looks like one minister choosing to prioritize formation over performance.

One school campus deciding to give students agency. One parish dropping a legacy event so they can invest in small groups. One DRE telling the truth about what's not working—and inviting others to help reimagine what might.

This is not a flashy rebrand. It's not a new program or an online campaign. It's a quiet revolution rooted in reality and hope. It's faithful ministers choosing to stop pretending and start planting. Not to tear everything down, but to prune what no longer bears fruit—so that something more true can grow.

You don't need to burn out to be brave. You don't need to go rogue to be faithful. You don't need to wait for a committee to validate your instinct that something deeper is needed. You just need to start. With the people in front of you. With the trust you've built. With the cracks in the system that are letting light in. With the Spirit already moving in the room, even if no one's noticed yet. Ministry is not a monument. It's a movement. And sometimes the movement is small, even hidden. But it's still real. And it still matters.

THE WORK STILL MATTERS

If your work feels hidden, you're in good company. The Gospels are built on hidden faithfulness. Joseph, obeying the angel in a dream. Mary, saying yes in silence. Jesus himself, living thirty unrecorded years in Nazareth before preaching a word. The Church was not born in headlines or grand strategy. It was born in small homes, whispered prayers, and unlikely trust. And so it continues.

The retreat you led that no one thanked you for. The student you walked with through grief. The sacrament you helped a teen rediscover. The late-night emails. The carefully phrased social media post that made sure no one felt shamed. The altar linens you ironed. The volunteers you called. The student who came back. The one who didn't—but still knew you cared. None of it is wasted.

Because the Kingdom is not built by metrics. It is built by mustard seeds. It is built by your quiet faithfulness, again and again, in places no one claps for and few people understand. You may not see the fruit. But the soil remembers. Grace has its own memory.

Conclusion

You are not failing because you're tired. You are not unworthy because your numbers are low. You are not alone because the room was half full. You are still here. And the work still matters.

Accompaniment Meditation III

THE HIDDEN LIFE OF THE MINISTER

Before anything else, take a breath. Close your eyes, if you can. Let the noise around you soften. Let the expectations fall away, just for a moment. You are not here to produce. You are not here to impress. You are here because you were called, and said yes. You are here because you stayed.

Ministry is often lived in obscurity. The most meaningful conversations are the ones no one else sees. The greatest sacrifices are made in silence. You prepare the prayer service that gets cancelled. You plan the retreat that only a handful attend. You offer a word of encouragement that lands without response. You show up, again and again, in the quiet, unnoticed spaces.

There's a deep loneliness in that sometimes. A sense that your efforts don't matter because they aren't being measured. A creeping suspicion that faithfulness without visibility might not be enough. The world counts clicks. The institution counts heads. You count the few who return, the one who opens up, the moment you sensed the Holy Spirit moving even if no one else seemed to notice. This is the hidden life of the minister.

It is patterned, whether we know it or not, on the hidden life of Christ. Thirty years of obscurity. Thirty years of labor, family, walking dusty roads, keeping holy days, living among neighbors who had no idea who he was. Only three years of public ministry—but decades of quiet faithfulness behind them.

Accompaniment Meditation III

Holiness is not built on platforms. It is built in kitchens, classrooms, chapels, and copy rooms. It is built in the silence after a student tells you they're struggling. In the patience it takes to answer a question you've heard a hundred times. In the choice to show up when you don't feel like it. In the prayers whispered between emails. In the decision to forgive the criticism that stung. The fruit of this life is slow. It ripens without fanfare. But it is real.

There is a reason we often feel unseen. Because much of what we do is not meant to be seen—not right away.[1] God is not in a hurry. He knows how to work in hiddenness. He is the Lord of mustard seeds, and yeast, and silent growth beneath the soil. Let yourself rest in that.

You do not have to prove your worth to God.[2] You do not have to manufacture transformation. You are not a spiritual content creator. You are a witness. A sower. A servant. You are part of something far deeper than you can measure. And when you feel the weight of invisibility again, remember this: God sees in secret. And what is grown in secret, He will one day bring to light.

So stay close. Stay rooted. Stay hidden, if you must. Because hidden is not forgotten. It's holy.

LETTING GO OF THE SCOREBOARD

Ministry tempts us to keep score. It starts subtly—just noticing who showed up, who stayed, who seemed moved. It creeps into our self-worth when we compare numbers from this year to last, this event to the one down the street. We begin to measure our faithfulness by someone else's applause, our effectiveness by someone else's metrics. And when the scoreboard doesn't favor us, we wonder whether we're doing something wrong. But Christ never asked us to count that way.

---

1. Matthew 6:4
2. While outside of the context of this work, see Max Weber's *Protestant Ethic and the Spirit of Capitalism* for an interesting discussion on how the osmosis of Puritan work ethic has pushed itself into much of the western culture, with implications for how we view our relationship to God.

Part III: What We're Really Called To

He never promised us packed rooms. He never said, "Blessed are those whose events go viral." He said, "Feed my sheep." Not, "Report back how many came to dinner." He said, "Make disciples," not "impress spectators." The Gospel isn't a strategy. It's a seed. And seeds take time.

Sometimes we plant and someone else waters. Sometimes we water what someone else planted. Sometimes we tend soil that looks barren. Sometimes we harvest what we didn't sow. We are not called to own the outcomes. We are called to be faithful in the task. There's a freedom in that.

It means you don't have to outdo yourself every year. You don't have to recreate the perfect retreat or rebrand the ministry to match current trends. You don't have to chase the applause or fear the silence. You just have to say yes again. And again. And again.

The scoreboard is seductive because it gives the illusion of control. But it's not real. Souls don't grow on spreadsheets. Conversion doesn't follow quarterly trends. The deepest movements of grace are quiet, slow, and hidden—often invisible to us until years later, if ever.

And that's okay.

God is keeping a different kind of score: The small yes when you were tired. The conversation you didn't rush. The prayer you offered when no one knew. The act of love with no return. The refusal to give up. This is the scoreboard of the Kingdom. It cannot be published in a bulletin or captured in a photo. It lives in heaven's memory. So let go.

Let go of the pressure to prove. Let go of the fear that you're not doing enough. Let go of the illusion that you can gauge grace by visible success. And hold fast to what is real: The call. The fidelity. The God who sees in silence. He is not asking you to be impressive. He is asking you to be faithful. That is the only scoreboard that matters.

Accompaniment Meditation III

PRAYERS FOR THE ONES WHO STAY

Let us begin in stillness. Take a breath. Let it be honest. Let it carry the weight of all you have not said aloud.

You are tired. Not from laziness, but from love. Not from apathy, but from trying too hard for too long without being seen. You have carried programs on your back, students in your prayers, teams through conflict, and visions into spaces that did not know how to receive them. You have kept going—through canceled events, delayed decisions, shrinking rosters, and leadership changes.

You have held joy in one hand and disappointment in the other. You have smiled through meetings where your work was reduced to numbers. You have asked for help and received silence. You have shown up anyway. Let this be a space where your weariness is named, not judged. Let this be the place where your tired hope is safe.

Prayer for Weariness

God of the unthanked and the unseen,
You saw the widow's coin.
You noticed the sparrow.
You know the long hours and hidden labor of Your servants.
Be near to those who are barely holding on—not because they don't love You, but because they have loved You through too much silence.
Stay with us in the ache.
Stay with us in the tension between what we dreamed and what we live.
Stay with us as we breathe, weep, and begin to pray.
Amen.

Part III: What We're Really Called To

Naming the Hidden Faithfulness

God of the quiet labor,
We bring to You what no one else sees.
The chairs set up early and put away alone.
The names remembered from last year's confirmation class.
The coffee bought for a student who didn't say thank you.
The parents called, the rooms cleaned, the candles lit.
The lessons rewritten at the last minute because something didn't feel right.
You have seen every late-night email, every hallway conversation, every prayer whispered in the car on the way to a retreat.
You know the weight of carrying a student's story long after the event ends.
You know the cost of staying gentle in meetings that lack charity.
You know what it means to keep sowing seeds in soil no one else is tending.
This is not wasted work.
This is the work of Your Kingdom.
You chose fishermen, tentmakers, tax collectors—people without titles or platforms.
You still do.
You walk with those who prepare the way in small places.
You delight in the labor done without applause.
You are not impressed by metrics.
You are moved by mercy.
So we name what has gone unnamed:
The faithfulness of showing up when it's easier to disappear.
The choice to care again, even after disappointment.
The willingness to believe You are still working—even here.
Let this be our offering.
Not our achievements.
Not our numbers.
Just our presence.
Still here. Still Yours.
Amen.

Accompaniment Meditation III

A Prayer for Steadfastness

Lord,
I am tired of counting.
Tired of waiting for visible fruit.
Tired of wondering if it mattered.
So I place it in Your hands again.
The retreat that didn't fill.
The student who stopped showing up.
The meeting that felt like a waste.
The silence that followed my yes.
Let these not be failures in Your eyes.
Root me in the work that no one sees:
The gentle listening.
The second chances.
The hard forgiveness.
The staying power.
Teach me to love the unseen seeds.
To trust in Your quiet growth.
To believe that fidelity—not applause, not numbers, not recognition is the real measure of my call.
Keep soft my heart.
Don't let disappointment calcify it.
Don't let cynicism grow in its corners.
Don't let me become efficient at the cost of love.
When I am tempted to chase relevance, call me back to presence.
When I am tempted to despair, call me back to hope.
When I am tempted to perform, call me back to You.
Steady my hands for the long work.
The work that does not end in a semester.
The work that doesn't post well on Instagram.
The work that might never be named, but which echoes in the lives of others in ways only You can trace.
You have not called me to be the answer.
You have called me to be faithful.
So I will rise again today.

I will show up again today.
I will serve again today.
Not because it is easy.
Not because I am enough.
But because You are.
Amen.

Petition for Renewal

Lord of the harvest,
We are tired—and we are still willing.
We do not ask for ease, but we ask for energy.
We do not ask for results, but we ask for renewal.
Give us endurance, when routines feel rote and the work grows thin.
When we doubt whether it's worth it.
When we wonder if anyone sees.
When we are tempted to stop hoping.
Give us vision, not just to see what's broken, but to imagine what could be rebuilt.
Help us remember why we said yes in the first place—and help us say yes again, this time with eyes open.
Give us companionship, the kind that steadies our steps when we want to walk away.
The kind that listens without fixing, that prays when we cannot find the words.
Send us friends who share the weight.
Send us mentors who still believe.
Send us students whose questions pull us closer to You.
Lord, we know we were not made to carry this alone.
We know the Cross was never meant to be a solo burden.
So we ask for a renewal not of systems or programs, but of spirit.
Let joy return—not as a performance, but as a sign that grace is still flowing.
Let love deepen—not as sentiment, but as the strength to keep showing up.

Accompaniment Meditation III

Let Christ remain—not as an idea, but as the One who walks beside us in every hallway,
every meeting, every moment when we wonder if this still matters.
You are the vine. We are the branches.
Root us again.
Still here. Still Yours.
Amen.

BENEDICTION FOR THE ROAD

I don't know where this finds you. Maybe you're energized, brimming with new ideas and hopeful plans. Maybe you're tired, nursing wounds that haven't quite healed. Maybe you're somewhere in between—showing up, still faithful, but worn. Wherever you are, I want you to hear this from someone who knows the weight: Your presence matters.

Not because of what you accomplish. Not because of how many students showed up, or how many events went smoothly, or whether the bulletin photo captured what really happened.

Your presence matters because you carry Christ with you. In your patience. In your perseverance. In the moments no one else sees—when you listen just a little longer, when you pray even when you're not sure it's working, when you forgive the hundredth small slight because the mission matters more than your pride. You are not invisible to the One who called you.

And I pray—

That when the work feels too quiet, you will remember that seeds grow in silence.

That when the calendar feels relentless, you will remember that rest is holy, not optional.

That when your effort goes unrecognized, you will remember that God is not counting the likes—He is counting the love.

I pray you find people who remind you who you are when ministry tries to flatten you into a role. I pray you receive encouragement that doesn't feel like performance coaching. I pray you

Part III: What We're Really Called To

have moments—small, surprising, grace-filled—that remind you why you said yes in the first place.

And I pray that even when you question it all, you'll know you're not alone. You are part of something bigger. Not a machine. Not a brand. A body. A mission. A communion of saints still being formed.

You are not the savior of your parish. You are not the solution to your school's decline. You are a witness. And that is enough.

So as you close this book and return to whatever comes next, I hope you walk lighter—not because the burden is gone, but because you remember Someone carries it with you.

Still here.

Still faithful.

Still worth it.

I'm praying for you.

And I'm walking with you.

Bibliography

Hart, Thomas. *The Art of Christian Listening*. Mahwah, NJ: Paulist, 1980.

Pontifical Council for the Promotion of the New Evangelization. *Directory for Catechesis*. Washington, DC: United States Conference of Catholic Bishops, 2020.

Pope Francis. Apostolic Exhortation on the Joy of the Gospel, *Evangelii Gaudium*. November 24, 2013. https://www.vatican.va/content/francesco/en/apost_exhortations/documents/papa-francesco_esortazione-ap_20131124_evangelii-gaudium.html

Pope John Paul II. Post-Synodal Apostolic Exhortation *Christifideles Laici*. December 30, 1988. https://www.vatican.va/content/john-paul-ii/en/apost_exhortations/documents/hf_jp-ii_exh_30121988_christifideles-laici.html

Pope Paul VI. Apostolic Exhortation. *Evangelii Nuntiandi*. December 8, 1975. https://www.vatican.va/content/paul-vi/en/apost_exhortations/documents/hf_p-vi_exh_19751208_evangelii-nuntiandi.html

Saint Mary's Press & The Center for Applied Research in the Apostolate. *Going, Going, Gone: The Dynamics of Disaffiliation in Young Catholics*. Winona, MN: Saint Mary's Press, 2017.

Second Vatican Council. Dogmatic Constitution on the Church, *Lumen Gentium*. November 1964.
https://www.vatican.va/archive/hist_councils/ii_vatican_council/documents/vat-ii_const_19641121_lumen-gentium_en.html

Second Vatican Council. Pastoral Constitution on the Church in the Modern World. *Gaudium et Spes*. December 7, 1965. https://www.vatican.va/archive/hist_councils/ii_vatican_council/documents/vat-ii_const_19651207_gaudium-et-spes_en.html

Springtide Research Institute. *Belonging: Reconnecting America's Loneliest Generation*. Bloomington, MN: Springtide Research Institute, 2020.

———. *The State of Religion and Young People 2020: Relational Authority*. Bloomington, MN: Springtide Research Institute, 2020.

Bibliography

United States Conference of Catholic Bishops. *Co-Workers in the Vineyard of the Lord: A Resource for Guiding the Development of Lay Ecclesial Ministry.* Washington, DC: 2005.

———. *Listen, Teach, Send: A National Pastoral Framework for Ministries with Youth and Young Adults.* Our Sunday Visitor, 2024.

Weber, Max. *The Protestant Work Ethic and the Spirit of Capitalism.* Translated by Talcott Parsons. New York: Charles Scribner's Sons, 1950.

www.ingramcontent.com/pod-product-compliance
Lightning Source LLC
Chambersburg PA
CBHW071213160426
43196CB00011B/2289